THE BOOK OF THE B.S.A. THREE WHEELER

A COMPLETE GUIDE FOR OWNERS
AND PROSPECTIVE PURCHASERS

BY

HAROLD JELLEY

SECOND EDITION

1935

Copyright 2018 by: www.VelocePress.com

INTRODUCTION

Welcome to the world of digital publishing ~ the book you now hold in your hand, was printed using the latest state of the art digital technology. The advent of print-on-demand has forever changed the publishing process, never has information been so accessible and it is our hope that this book serves your informational needs for years to come. If this is your first exposure to digital publishing, we hope that you are pleased with the results. Many more titles of interest to the classic automobile and motorcycle enthusiast, collector and restorer are available via our website at www.VelocePress.com. We hope that you find this title as interesting as we do.

NOTE FROM THE PUBLISHER

The information presented is true and complete to the best of our knowledge. All recommendations are made without any guarantees on the part of the author or the publisher, who also disclaim all liability incurred with the use of this information.

TRADEMARKS

We recognize that some words, model names and designations, for example, mentioned herein are the property of the trademark holder. We use them for identification purposes only. This is not an official publication.

INFORMATION ON THE USE OF THIS PUBLICATION

This manual is an invaluable resource for those interested in performing their own maintenance. However, in today's information age we are constantly subject to changes in common practice, new technology, availability of improved materials and increased awareness of chemical toxicity. As such, it is advised that the user consult with an experienced professional prior to undertaking any procedure described herein. While every care has been taken to ensure correctness of information, it is obviously not possible to guarantee complete freedom from errors or omissions or to accept liability arising from such errors or omissions. Therefore, any individual that uses the information contained within, or elects to perform or participate in do-it-yourself repairs or modifications acknowledges that there is a risk factor involved and that the publisher or its associates cannot be held responsible for personal injury or property damage resulting from the use of the information or the outcome of such procedures.

WARNING!

One final word of advice, this publication is intended to be used as a reference guide, and when in doubt the reader should consult with a qualified technician.

PREFACE

THE BOOK OF THE B.S.A. THREE WHEELER is published with a view to assisting owners in the solution of all the difficulties, mechanical and otherwise, which are likely to arise. To the beginner some assistance is essential, if he is to obtain the best service from his car. The driver of experience, also, will find explicit information on a number of points which frequently puzzle the adept.

The B.S.A. Three Wheeler is primarily a sports car. It is all the more important, therefore, that the engine and component parts should be kept in perfect condition, if efficient sports performance is to be maintained.

The chapters on Maintenance and Overhaul, Lubrication, the Electrical Equipment and Care of Tyres contain all the information which is necessary to ensure perfect running order throughout the life of the car. The purchaser of a secondhand model, also, will find he can improve the performance of his car out of all recognition by following the advice given in these chapters. The directions given are those which have been proved by experience to be most effective under all conditions.

I shall be very glad to receive suggestions from readers on the running and maintenance of the Beeza with a view to incorporating them in future editions of the book.

Acknowledgment is due to the B.S.A. Company, Ltd., for supplying many blocks and photographs, and also for the opportunity of testing one of the latest Special Sports Models.

H. J.

1935.

CONTENTS

CHAP.		PAGE
	PREFACE	
I.	THE RANGE OF MODELS	1
II.	LICENCES, INSURANCE, AND LAW	10
III.	THE FOUR-STROKE ENGINE EXPLAINED	16
IV.	ON THE ROAD WITH THE THREE WHEELER	21
V.	MAINTENANCE AND OVERHAUL	32
VI.	LUBRICATION	80
VII.	THE ELECTRICAL EQUIPMENT	92
VIII.	CARE OF TYRES	106
	APPENDIX	113
	INDEX	120

THE BOOK OF THE B.S.A. THREE WHEELER

CHAPTER I

THE RANGE OF MODELS

FRONT wheel drive, all wheel braking, interchangeable wheels, three speeds and reverse, electric starter and car type controls are standard on all models, and the performance put up by these cars is amazing, considering the low price of from £100 and a tax of £4. In fact, the performance is well above that of the average small car, having far superior acceleration, with a much better top gear performance on hills. There is ample room for two people (or in the family model—two adults and two children) to travel in comfort, and in wet weather there is ample protection for all to ride under cover.

Six models are marketed, four employing the two-cylinder engine, and the remainder fitted with the four-cylinder, side-valve sports engine. The twin-cylinder models have an extremely good performance to their credit, but for those who require a really fast, economical and sporting car, the four-cylinder models are undoubtedly the better proposition. Front wheel drive which, as already stated, is standard on all six models, enables quickly detachable and interchangeable wheels to be fitted, considerably reduces tyre wear, and with well-balanced braking, reduces the risk of skidding.

The specification of the models is given below, while the price is given at the end of this chapter.

THE TWIN-CYLINDER MODEL

Frame and Suspension. The engine and transmission are supported on a channel section steel frame of great strength. The front wheels are independently sprung, each being supported on four quarter elliptic springs which take the place of the axle casing in an ordinary rear-driven car. The frame side members converge at the back on to a bracket at the end of a strong steel tube. This bracket supports a cantilever on which the rear wheel is mounted. The inner end of this cantilever carries a quarter elliptic spring projecting inside the tube on to which the front end of the spring abuts through a felt-lined steel slipper. The spring is attached to the slipper by a Silentbloc bearing which requires no lubrication. The felt lining of the slipper is saturated with grease before assembly, and therefore requires only occa-

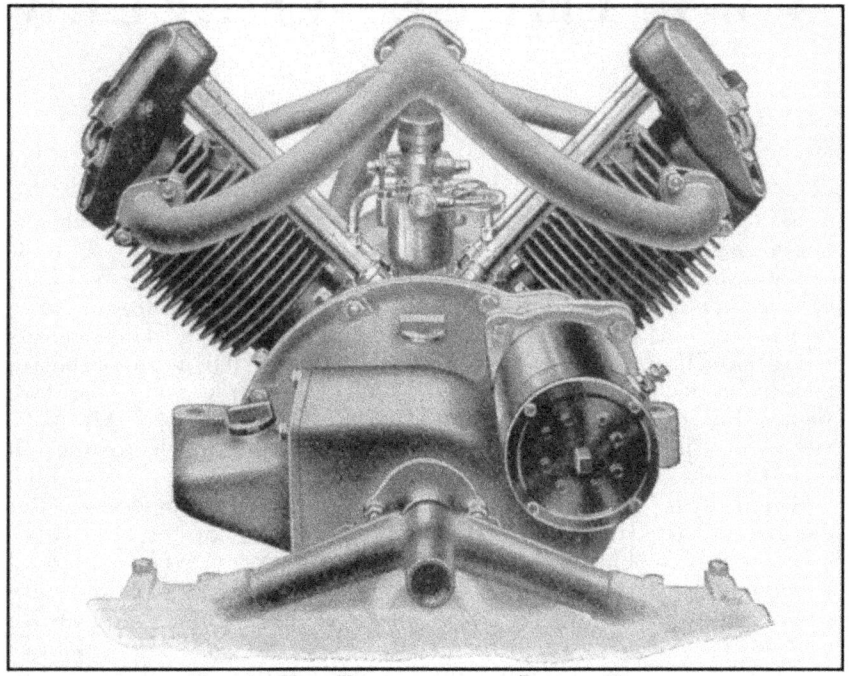

FIG. 1. THE TWIN-CYLINDER POWER UNIT

sional lubrication, provision for which is made by means of a grease gun nipple on the side of the tube.

The wheels are of heavy gauge 19 in. by 3 in. rims with high tensile steel spokes, and are fitted with 4·00–19 Dunlop tyres. As already stated, the wheels are quickly detachable and interchangeable, and a spare wheel is included in the specification, this being fixed on the side of the car.

Engine. The power unit is a 90° vee-twin (Fig. 1) with a bore and stroke of 85 m.m. by 90 m.m. respectively, and the total capacity is 1,021 c.c. A Solex carburettor is fitted and this has an exhaust hot spot. Slow running adjustment is provided on the steering column and a pedal accelerator is employed on all models, thus conforming with car practice. The petrol tank holds $4\frac{1}{2}$ gal. and a reserve tap is fitted. Coil ignition is employed and the

THE RANGE OF MODELS

control lever is fitted on the steering column. The valves, which are of the overhead type, are of special steel, operated by enclosed and properly lubricated rockers and rods. The big-end bearings are lubricated by special oil feed direct to the bearings. Roller bearings are employed on crankshaft and connecting rod big ends, and the fly-wheel is of steel.

Engine Lubrication. Five pints of oil are contained in a sump that is integral with the crankcase, and in which is a submerged gear type pump driven by worm gear from the crankshaft. A dip stick is fitted for measuring the oil level in the sump, and the oil pressure is maintained by the pump and automatically controlled by a by-pass valve. Oil is delivered to the big-end bearings, cylinder walls, and the timing gear, the supply being controlled by a valve on the timing cover. This valve is correctly set during the works test and normally requires no further adjustment.

Transmission. The clutch, which is of the floating plate type with cork inserts, is of large diameter, and is mounted in the fly-wheel and runs in oil. The gearbox contains three forward speeds and reverse, the ratios being 5·16, 7·75, 16·8, and 20·7 respectively. Worm gear drive to the front axle with spur type differential is employed, and from the differential the drive is transmitted to the front wheels through strong flexible couplings and universal joints.

Chassis Lubrication. Grease gun lubrication is provided for all chassis parts requiring this attention. They are very few in number and are all accessible (see page 88).

Brakes. The brakes are of the internal expanding type and of ample size. That on the differential controls both front wheels, and there is a brake on the rear wheel. The pedal controls all brakes simultaneously, and retards the car on all wheels, thus minimizing the possibility of skids. The hand brake operates on the rear wheel only and is intended primarily as a parking brake, but it can be used in addition to the pedal at any time (see page 69 for maintenance hints).

Miscellaneous Equipment. Speedometer, electric horn, oil gauge, ammeter, screenwiper, full kit of tools including jack, wheel brace, tyre pump, grease gun, and a licence holder, completes the specification.

THE FOUR-CYLINDER MODEL

Engine. This engine (see Fig. 2) employs side-by-side valves with high-efficiency detachable cylinder head. The bore and stroke is 60 m.m. by 95 m.m. (total capacity 1,075 c.c.) respectively, and the Treasury rating is 8·9 h.p., the tax being £4. The large diameter two-bearing crankshaft, short and free from whip, is mounted on ball and roller journal bearings. The cylinder block and crankcase is one casting, ensuring greater rigidity and perfect alinement. The silent timing gear with wide cams on large diameter camshaft, is driven from the crankshaft by duplex chain.

Lubrication. A gear type pump driven by skew gears from the camshaft is employed, and the pump draws oil from engine sump (capacity 1 gal.) and delivers it under high pressure to the big-end bearings through the hollow crankshaft, and also to the tappet gallery, where lubrication is provided for the tappets, cams, and

FIG. 2. OFFSIDE VIEW OF FOUR-CYLINDER POWER UNIT

camshaft bearings. An oil pressure gauge is fitted on the instrument panel.

Carburettor. This is a Solex self-starting carburettor, and the easy starting and slow running controls are operated from the instrument panel (see page 62 for maintenance and overhauling hints).

Clutch. The clutch is of the multi-plate type having two light alloy discs with cork inserts, running in oil. It is particularly sweet in action, entirely free from slip, and owing to its light weight ensures very rapid gear changing.

Gearbox. This is a B.S.A. product and has three speeds and reverse, silent double-helical constant mesh gears. The three forward gear ratios are: 5·16, 7·75, 16·8, reverse gear being 20·7.

Electrical Equipment. Lucas equipment is standard on all models and the coil ignition system on this model is fitted with automatic spark advance which has to be tried to be appreciated. There are five lamps employed on this model, all of which are chromium plated, and a dipper control is fitted to the headlights.

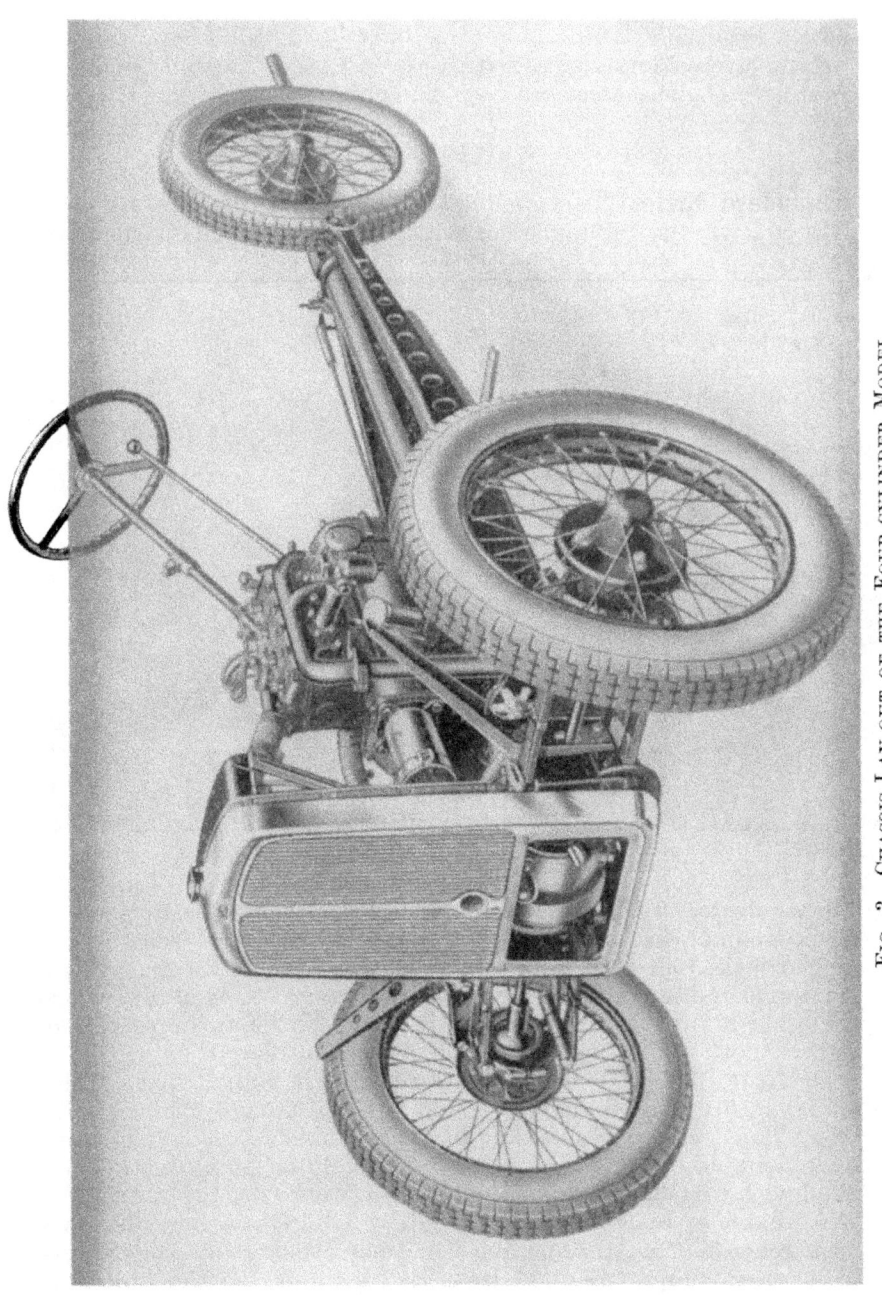

Fig. 3. Chassis Lay-out of the Four-cylinder Model

6   THE BOOK OF THE B.S.A. THREE WHEELER

Sports type side lamps, combined stop and tail lamp, six volt system with dynamo, self-starter and large capacity battery completes the specification.

BODYWORK

Standard Model. This model (Fig. 4) has a black fabric body with red wheels, folding hood with sidescreens, and safety glass

Fig. 4. The Standard Model

flat windscreen. The five-lamp set on this model is finished in black enamel to conform with the general colour scheme. A hinged locker lid at rear of car gives access to the luggage compartment and a quickly detachable rear guard to facilitate wheel changing is fitted. The pneumatic upholstery for the seat is of leather cloth while the fittings are chromium plated.

De Luxe Model. The aluminium panelled body fitted to this model is finished in lavender and grey, dual grey, black with ivory, blue, red, or green. The wings are finished in black enamel. A detachable hood with sidescreens, or folding hood can be supplied with this model. The five-lamp set is chromium-plated and a large diameter exhaust pipe is fitted, which gives a very nice note on a generous throttle opening. A hinged locker lid gives access to luggage compartment at rear, and a quickly detachable rear guard facilitates wheel removal (see Fig. 45). The pneumatic upholstery for the seat is of leather cloth and is finished in dark blue. All bright parts are chromium-plated.

Family De Luxe Model. This model (Fig. 5) has an aluminium panelled body, and is finished in cellulose in black and blue, dual grey, grey and lavender, black with ivory, red, or green, the wings being finished in black enamel. A folding hood with side-screens is fitted and all four passengers are amply protected from rain. The five-lamp set is finished in chromium-plating. The

Fig. 5. The Family de Luxe Model

driver's seat is adjustable, and the front passenger's seat is hinged to allow easy access to the rear seats.

Special Sports Model. As on the model described above, an aluminium panelled body is fitted on this model and has a cellulose finish. Alternate colour schemes are available, viz. lavender and grey, dual grey, and black with ivory, blue, red, or green. A detachable hood with sidescreens is fitted, which can be stored in the locker when not in use. The five-lamp set is chromium-plated and instructions are given in a later chapter with regard to the care of this special plating. As on the other models, a hinged locker lid gives easy access to the luggage compartment.

8   THE BOOK OF THE B.S.A. THREE WHEELER

Pneumatic upholstery is provided for the seat and one can travel long distances in comfort without feeling "saddle sore."

Four-cylinder De Luxe Model. An aluminium panelled body with cellulose finish is fitted to this model (Fig. 6) and alternate

FIG. 6. THE FOUR-CYLINDER DE LUXE MODEL

FIG. 7. THE TWO-CYLINDER MODEL WITH RICE CARAVAN

colour schemes are available, and these are as follows: Black and ivory, dual grey or lavender and grey. The hood and sidescreens are detachable and can be stored in the locker when not required. Fort Dunlop tyres are fitted, and Chapter VIII gives many useful hints and tips with regard to the care of tyres. The remainder of the specification is similar to that given for the special sports model.

THE RANGE OF MODELS

THE B.S.A. WITH A CARAVAN

Very few people realize that a three-wheeler is suitable for towing a caravan, but the caravan shown in Fig. 7 was towed throughout Devonshire and the car (two-cylinder model) behaved very well. This surely speaks for itself and needs no further recommendation from me.

The caravan shown is the Rice Standard Model, and full particulars can be obtained from Rice Caravans. These caravans may also be hired for a reasonable charge.

THE RANGE AT A GLANCE

Model	Engine	Price
		£
Standard	Twin-cylinder	100
De Luxe	Twin-cylinder	108
Family de Luxe	Twin-cylinder	110
Special Sports	Twin-cylinder	115
Four-cylinder Model	Four-cylinder water-cooled	125
Four-cylinder De Luxe	Four-cylinder water-cooled	128

CHAPTER II

LICENCES, INSURANCE, AND LAW

IT is very seldom, nowadays, that the purchaser of a new car has to bother with such matters as the licensing of the car and other details. This is more often carried out by the agent from whom the car is purchased, but for the benefit of those who have to do this themselves, the following paragraphs should be of assistance.

The law and insurance are two very important items and the reader should make himself familiar with the law as it affects him. There may come a time when you are in need of advice, and the section on legal matters is included so that the reader can see at a glance exactly what laws have been made and how they affect him.

The Driving Licence. This costs 5s. per annum and expires twelve months from the date it was taken out. Every driver of a mechanically-propelled vehicle must be in possession of a driving licence while driving such a vehicle. Sixteen is the minimum age for a licence to drive a three wheeler.

Application for a licence to drive must be made to the offices of the town or county council in which the applicant resides. These municipal authorities will provide the appropriate form of application which must be completed and returned to the council with the necessary fee of 5s. The possession of a driving licence is no proof of driving ability: indeed, it is compulsory that one takes out the licence before receiving any tuition in the driving of the car. A declaration as to physical fitness must be made by every applicant for a driving licence. This declaration must be in the form prescribed by the authorities, and it must state whether or not the applicant is suffering from any disease or physical disability which would be likely to render it dangerous to drive. Application for a licence may be made either personally at the municipal offices or through the post. If a driving licence should become lost a duplicate may be obtained on payment of 1s.

A licence is non-transferable, and the authorities do not notify the holder when his licence is due for renewal, the responsibility of taking out a renewal resting entirely with the holder.

The holder must sign the licence in the space provided before attempting to drive. This should be done immediately it is obtained. This also applies to a renewal of the licence.

LICENCES, INSURANCE, AND LAW

A police officer may at any time stop a motorist, and ask to see his or her driving licence without giving any reason for so doing. If unable immediately to produce the licence, the driver cannot be convicted of an offence if, within *five days* of the request for production, the licence is produced in person at any police station he may specify.

A police officer is not allowed to take note of any endorsements which may have been entered in the licence on the back pages. These endorsements, if any, are a record of any motoring offences of which the motorist has been convicted. In some cases, although the motorist may have been found guilty by the magistrate, no order is made by them that the licence shall be endorsed.

When the Court has ordered the licence to be endorsed, it must be produced in Court within *five days* or such longer time that the Court may determine. If not the holder of a licence, but subsequently obtaining one, he must produce it to the Court within *five days*. Failure in either case entails automatic suspension of the licence until produced.

If any person during the period of disqualification applies for or obtains a driving licence, or drives a motor vehicle, he is liable to imprisonment up to six months or to a fine of £50, or to both such imprisonment and fine. Such proceedings can be taken within six months of the date of the offence, or within a period which does not exceed three months from the date on which it came to the knowledge of the prosecutor, or one year from the offence, whichever period is the longer.

The holder of a licence which has been endorsed is entitled (a) on renewal; or (b) at any time on payment of 5s. to receive a new licence free from endorsements provided he has not had any conviction endorsed during a continuous period of not less than three years since the last endorsement and expiry of any period of disqualification.

Particulars of all endorsements or disqualifications are forwarded by the Court to the authorities who granted the licence and in whose area the holder resides. Where disqualification occurs, the Court forward the licence to the authority that issued the licence, who retain it until disqualification expires and the driver has made a request in writing for its return.

Renewing the Driving Licence. Upon the expiration of the licence at the end of twelve months, it will be necessary to complete a form for the application of renewal of driving licence and send this, together with the fee of 5s. to the appropriate local council offices from which the licence was originally obtained. Strictly speaking, one is then not allowed to drive because one is not in possession of one's licence. It will usually be found, however, that if some proof is carried, such as a copy of any letter which may have been sent to the council, requesting the renewal of the licence, or the counterfoil of the postal order (if payment was made in this way), it will satisfy the police, should they wish to see the driver's licence. It is a good plan, however, to apply for renewal of the licence a week or so before the date the licence actually expires. Better still, the driver should call at the licensing authority's offices in person, when a renewal will be issued without delay. (This last sentence should not be taken literally, however, as one occasionally has to wait as long as 30 min.)

Registration of the Car. Before the owner may take a car on the road it must be taxed, registered, and fitted with registration number plates, one at the front and one at the rear.

The tax on a B.S.A. is £4 per annum and commences on the 1st January and expires on the 31st December. A quarterly tax is obtainable, the quarter days being 24th March, 30th June, 30th September, and 31st December. Alternatively, the car may be taxed from any day the owner wishes, the tax in this case to run to the end of the year.

Before a new car can be registered, the authorities will require some proof that the vehicle is brand new and demand production of the manufacturer's or agent's sales delivery note, or the agent's invoice, either of which should bear the engine and any other number by which the car can be proved not to have been previously registered. Also, the authorities will require to see the certificate of insurance issued to the owner by the insurance company. These, and other details which the authorities will ask for, must be supplied on the appropriate form of application for a licence. In return for this form and the amount of the tax, the owner will receive a registration book and the licence. The latter must always be carried in the licence holder provided on the near side of the car. There is no necessity to carry the registration book, but the owner will be advised to read the instructions printed thereon. Upon the expiration of the licence a renewal can be obtained either from the council with whom the car is registered or from any post office authorized for this purpose. Fourteen days' grace is allowed, but a post office cannot grant a renewal after the fourteen days' grace has expired. This must be obtained from the authorities referred to above.

If the registration book is lost, a new one can be obtained on payment of a fee of 5s. In the event of a duplicate being issued and the original subsequently found, return the original to the authority from whom it was obtained. If any alteration in the car, e.g. change of colour, or different type of body, which will affect the particulars previously registered, notify (in writing) the council of the alteration and forward the book for amendment.

If transferring ownership (1) deliver the book to the new owner;

LICENCES, INSURANCE, AND LAW 13

(2) notify the change, in writing, to the council whose name appears last in the book, also the index mark, and registration number, the make and class of vehicle and the name and address of the new owner.

If you change your address, enter particulars of new address in the space provided in the book and forward it to the council with which the car is registered.

INSURANCE

Before venturing on the road with a B.S.A you are now compelled to take out a third party insurance policy. In addition to the usual policy, or cover note, the insurance company will hand to the owner a certificate of insurance in the prescribed form, and, as already stated, when applying for the car licence, the applicant must—by production of the certificate or otherwise—satisfy the licensing authority that the necessary cover against third party risks will be in force at the time the car licence becomes operative.

There is a very large number of insurance companies catering for motorists, and these are divided into two classes, i.e. **tariff** and **non-tariff**. Full information regarding rates can be obtained on application to the insurance companies.

A Comprehensive Policy. This type of policy is the one which readers are urged to take out, and the benefits are given below.

Loss of or Damage to Car. This covers transit by sea between any Ports in Great Britain, Ireland, the Isle of Man, or the Channel Islands. The exceptions are: loss of use, depreciation, wear and tear, mechanical or electrical breakdowns, failures or breakages, damage to tyres.

The insurance company bears the reasonable cost of removing the car from the scene of the accident to the nearest repairers, and similarly, the cost of delivery to the owner after repairs. Repairs, up to a reasonable amount, may be executed without the consent of the company, provided that a detailed estimate is previously obtained.

Liability to the Public. Claims by the public, including passengers, for personal injury or damage to property, including animals, caused by the car. The policy also indemnifies under this section: the insured while driving a private car or motor-cycle not belonging to him: relatives or friends not entitled to indemnity under any other policy while driving the insured car with the owner's knowledge and consent.

Injury to Owner. Personal injuries sustained in direct connection with the insured car while travelling in other private cars: death, £1,000; loss of two limbs or sight of both eyes, £500; loss of one limb or one eye, £250.

Medical Expenses. Where compensation is paid under the provision of compulsory insurance, and where to the knowledge of the insurer a third party has received hospital treatment, the insurer shall also pay to the hospital a sum not exceeding £25 for each person so treated. This obligation does not apply where a charge has already been made by the hospital.

THE LAW AND THE MOTORIST

Accidents (What to do). The first thing to do, in the event of any person being injured, is to obtain medical assistance and a policeman. This may in some circumstances be rather difficult, should the accident occur in some out-of-the-way place, but it is usually possible to find a telephone within at least a mile from any spot in England, at any rate.

Having done all that is possible in this connection, take the names and addresses of all available witnesses, particularly any disinterested parties. Get the policeman to take note of the positions of the damaged vehicles, and of any marks on the road which may be of assistance at a later date.

Do not omit to report the matter to your insurance company within twenty-four hours from the time of the accident: also advise your motoring association. Should a policeman not be on the spot the accident must be reported at any police station within twenty-four hours. Do not deal with any correspondence yourself. This should be posted to your insurance company, road association, or solicitor, as the case may be. Never offer any money to an injured person or to a witness at any time, as this may be taken as admitting liability.

Address. If you are accused of driving recklessly, dangerously or carelessly, you must give your name and address to any person having reasonable ground for requiring the information. If you refuse, or give a false name and address, you are guilty of an offence.

Arrest. A police officer, whether in uniform or not, who observes you commit the offence of reckless, dangerous, or careless driving, may arrest you without warrant, unless you give your name and address or produce your driving licence for examination.

It is not generally known that, under the Highways Act, 1835, a person who sees a motorist driving furiously to the danger of the public may arrest the motorist without a warrant.

Pedestrian Crossings. In an endeavour to reduce the number of road accidents, pedestrian crossings have been instituted. These crossing places for foot passengers are indicated by means of white lines, "Belisha beacons," metal studs, etc., as prescribed

LICENCES, INSURANCE, AND LAW

for the purpose by regulations of the Minister of Transport. Each local authority decides which method they propose to adopt, but it must be one of those authorized.

Drivers approaching a crossing are to proceed at a speed that will enable them, if required, to stop before reaching the crossing. Where the crossing is not controlled by a police officer or light signals, pedestrians have precedence over all vehicular traffic at these crossings. Drivers are not to stop on any crossing unless it is necessary to do so to avoid accident.

Driving Test. A driving test is provided for in the case of all new holders of driving licences, but this regulation does not apply to a person who held a driving licence before the 1st April, 1934. The form of the test will include such matters as examination in the Highway Code; starting a car, overtaking and backing the car within a limited space. Full regulations will be issued by the Minister of Transport. New licence holders are liable to be called upon to pass the specified test during the period of the licence.

Speed Limit. This regulation is now in force, and the general speed limit has been fixed at thirty miles an hour in built-up areas. A "built-up area" is defined as a length of road in which a system of street lighting is maintained by lamps not more than two hundred yards apart. Suitable signs have been erected in areas in which the speed limit is to be enforced. It must be remembered, however, that in certain areas, such as the Royal and municipal parks, there are definite limits to the speed of road vehicles.

Driving Off the Highway. Driving without lawful authority on to common land, moor land, or any land forming part of a road, except for a distance of 15 yd. for the purpose of parking, is prohibited. If, however, a vehicle is driven off the highway for purpose of saving life, extinguishing fire, or meeting a similar emergency, the driver will not be convicted. This legislation does not prejudice any local by-laws, or affect the law of trespass, and confers no actual right to park a vehicle on any land.

Horn. When a vehicle is stationary on the highway, the horn must not be used except when such use is necessary on the grounds of safety. Under a recent order the horn must not be sounded between the hours of 11.30 p.m. and 7.30 a.m.

Traffic Lights. There have been many cases recently where motorists have been summoned for not obeying the traffic lights. More often than not, their answer has been that they "thought that the amber light meant start." Amber and red means "prepare to start," while amber alone means "stop," and this signal should be obeyed.

CHAPTER III

THE FOUR-STROKE ENGINE

AFTER driving the car for some miles the thoughtful motorist will wonder exactly how the engine works, and this chapter is written for the benefit of this particular person. The majority of the readers of this book will already know exactly what work each part has to play, and I advise them not to read this chapter, as it must, of necessity, be elementary.

The Engine. The first part to be dealt with is the cylinder. This is of uniform diameter, and, when the detachable part is in position, is closed at one end, the interior being machined to a glass-like smoothness (a detachable head is not fitted to the air-cooled engine). The piston is also uniform in diameter, and also closed at one end, and this is made to fit the cylinder as closely as possible, but still allowing it to move easily therein. The combustion chamber is the space between the top of the piston and the cylinder head, and it is essential for this to be gas-tight, so that the explosive mixture may be compressed without loss. It is impossible to make the pistons themselves a gas-tight fit within the cylinder, for, if this was so, the friction set up would render movement difficult and, very soon, impossible; hence, the piston is fitted with what are known as piston rings. These are rings of springy iron, and are inserted into grooves in the outer wall of the piston. Owing to their natural expansion, they press closely against the cylinder wall; therefore, no gas can get past them. When the engine is working, the piston moves up and down in the cylinder, but before the power developed can be utilized for propelling the automobile, it is necessary to convert this movement into a rotary one. A main- or crankshaft is fitted in the crankcase, this being constructed with the necessary number of crankpins, one for each cylinder. The piston is connected to the crankpin by means of a connecting rod, which is fitted with suitable bearings at each end, so that as the piston works up and down the motion rotates the crankshaft. On the crankshaft is mounted a fly-wheel, the object of which is to store up the energy developed by the engine, so that the rotary movement of the crankshaft may be continued steadily and jerks obviated.

The explosive mixture, a mixture of fuel vapour and air, is induced to enter the combustion chamber through an inlet valve, while the exits of the products of combustion—carbon dioxide and water vapour—are expelled through the exhaust valve. The

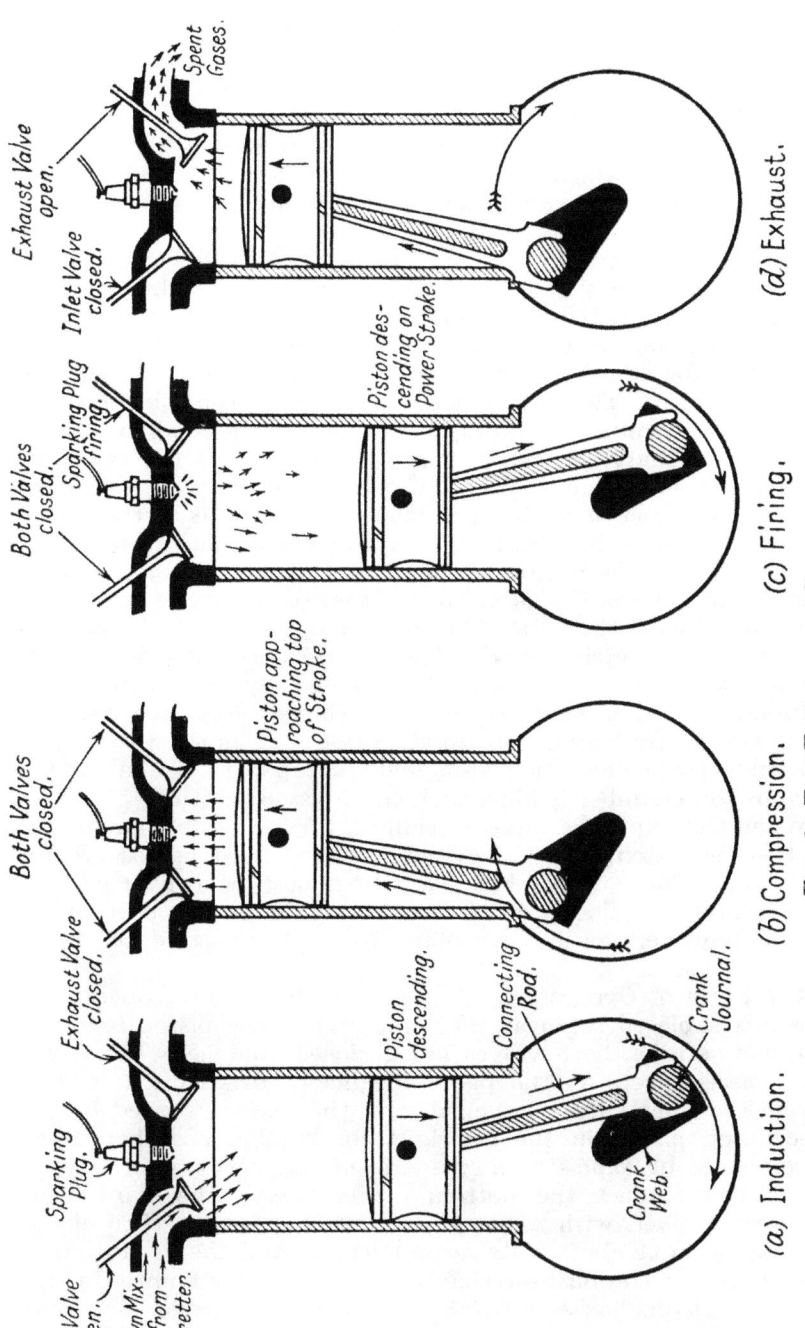

Fig. 8. THE FOUR-STROKE CYCLE

(a) Induction. (b) Compression. (c) Firing. (d) Exhaust.

(The above shows the operation of the O.H.V. engine. The principles of the side-valve engine are the same.)

valves are opened and closed by means of tappets, these being actuated by a camshaft which carries the necessary number of cams or protrusions. As the cam comes into action the tappet is forced upwards, which action raises the valve. The valve closes after the cam comes out of action by means of a strong spring which encircles the valve stem.

The " Otto " Cycle. The majority of engines are operated on what is termed the " Otto " principle, a principle which is adopted for the B.S.A. This type of engine is more generally known as the four-stroke, in that an explosion occurs in the cylinder only once for every four movements of the piston, i.e. two up and two down. This means that each valve, the inlet and the exhaust valve, must open only once for every second revolution of the crankshaft; hence, they are timed so that the camshaft revolves at half-engine speed. Generally, it may be said that the inlet valve is timed to open when the piston is at the top of its stroke, that is, nearest to the cylinder head, and closes when the piston is at the bottom of its stroke, while the exhaust valve opens when the piston is at the bottom of its stroke and closes when it reaches the top. The explosive mixture is ignited by means of an electric spark. The electric current which causes the spark at the plug points is supplied by the battery and induction coil. The spark is timed to occur once for every second revolution of the crankshaft, in the same way as the valves, and this takes place when the piston is at the top of its stroke and the combustion chamber is filled with compressed mixture.

When the explosive mixture is fired, a considerable amount of heat is generated, and the cylinder, piston, and valves become very hot. This surplus heat, which cannot be converted into power, must be dissipated; hence, the cylinders are surrounded by water-jackets, or large cooling fins in the case of the twin-cylinder model.

The Cycle of Operations. To describe the cycle of operations, it is advisable to begin at that stage when the piston is at the top of its stroke, both valves being closed, and here Fig. 8 will be of assistance. As the piston begins to descend on its first stroke the inlet valve is opened, and the suction caused by the descending piston in the gas-tight combustion chamber draws in a charge of explosive mixture from the carburettor. When the piston reaches the bottom of its travel, the combustion chamber is filled with mixture, and the inlet valve then closes. The piston next rises on its second stroke, and the mixture contained in the combustion chamber is compressed until by the time the piston has arrived at the top of the stroke—the compression stroke—a pressure of between 70 lb. and 80 lb. per square inch is obtained. At this moment a spark is caused to

THE FOUR-STROKE ENGINE

jump across the electrodes of the sparking plug, which ignites the mixture. As the mixture burns—it does not explode suddenly —the heat generated causes the gases to expand, and, therefore, the piston is forced down the cylinder on its third, or firing, stroke. When the bottom of the stroke is reached the combustion chamber is filled with inert gases, which must be expelled before a new

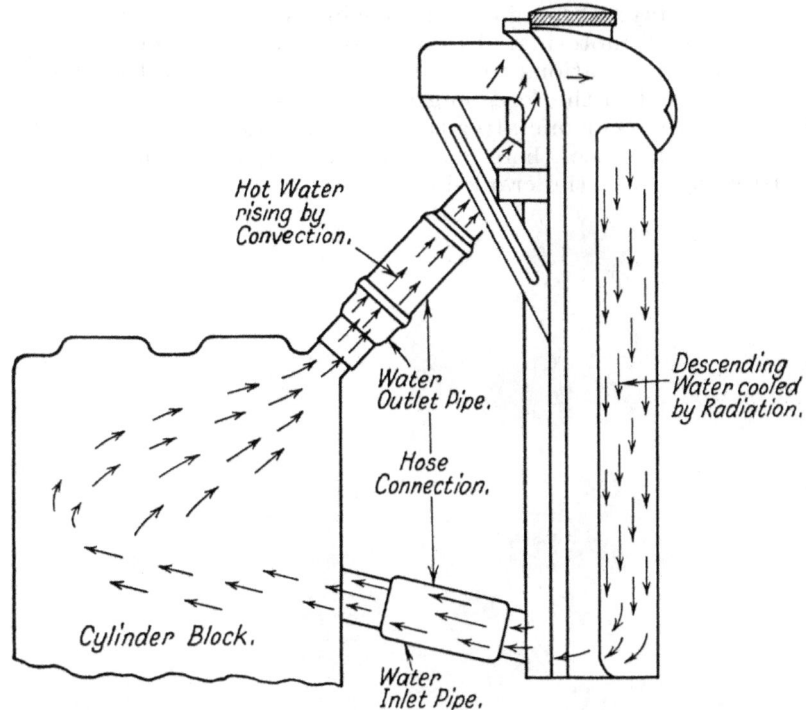

FIG. 9. THE THERMO-SIPHON ENGINE COOLING PRINCIPLE
(The above principle is dependent upon the physical property of hot water rising to be replaced by water cooled by the radiator, and so forming a regular cycle of operations.)

charge can be induced into the cylinder. As soon as the bottom of the firing stroke is reached, therefore, the exhaust valve is timed to open, so that as the piston ascends on its fourth stroke these products of combustion are forced out into the exhaust pipe, and finally to the atmosphere. At the termination of this stroke—the exhaust stroke—the exhaust valve closes and the inlet valve opens, so that a new charge of explosive mixture may be taken in by the engine.

The four strokes of the engine are, therefore—

Induction, piston descending and inlet valve opened.
Compression, piston ascending, both valves closed.

Firing, piston descending, both valves closed.

Exhaust, piston ascending, exhaust valve opened.

Only the third stroke of the cycle is a power, or impulse, stroke; the other three strokes are carried out by the power stored up in the fly-wheel. This is known as kinetic energy.

Multi-cylinder Engines. No cars are fitted with single cylinder engines to-day, although such machines were common in the early days of motoring. In the case of multi-cylinder engines, the cycle of operations in each cylinder is exactly the same as that described in the foregoing paragraphs, but the firing strokes are timed to occur one after the other, so that in a four-cylinder engine, for instance, there is a power or impulse stroke for every half-revolution of the crankshaft.

CHAPTER IV

ON THE ROAD WITH THE THREE WHEELER

DRIVING is a fine art and there are thousands of people driving to-day who, if a driving test were introduced, would immediately forfeit their licences through careless or inefficient driving. In this chapter, I hope to make clear to my readers, the necessary driving instructions as I consider they should be taught. Whether every reader will agree that my way is the best is another story.

Firstly, the controls should be gone over and, until you are sure that you can find the brakes and clutch pedals without fumbling about or looking down, don't attempt to drive off. We will go over the controls one by one so that you can get really familiar with them (by familiar, I don't mean careless).

Now take the driver's seat and have a look round. Probably the first thing you will notice is the gear lever. This is situated between the pedals and comes readily to the hand.

Next you will notice three pedals, that on the left is the clutch pedal, the middle and smallest is the accelerator pedal, while on the right is the footbrake pedal.

The clutch pedal, with the exception of the brakes, is the most important control on the car. Its object is to break the drive between the engine and gearbox. This is necessary, for example, when changing gear. Constant slipping of the clutch, however, should be avoided when possible. Some people imagine the clutch should be slipped to enable the car to crawl up a hill, or to enable the car to go slowly through traffic in top gear. The gearbox is supplied for occasions such as these, and full use should be made of the different gear ratios, particularly when running-in the engine.

The accelerator pedal regulates the supply of petrol gas to the engine, and thereby the speed and power of the car. It works with immediate effect, and any heavy, sudden acceleration or deceleration of the engine has to be transmitted to the car in the form of less or extra speed, and is bound to cause a strain on the clutch and other parts of the car responsible for turning the front wheels.

The function of the footbrake needs no explaining, but it may be as well to state here that the brakes should be treated with some respect. Fierce application in wet weather will most likely start a skid which the driver may have difficulty in correcting. Also, the tyres will soon show the effect of fierce braking.

Now turn your attention to the steering wheel, under which you will see the electric horn button, the head light dimming switch, the advance and retard control, and the slow-running control. (On the water-cooled models, the controls under the steering wheel are the horn button and dimming switch.)

The horn is operated by pressing the button and the head lights are dimmed by turning the small thumb lever to the right. The ignition is advanced by moving the control towards you and retarded by moving it away from you. (This is automatic on the water-cooled model.) The slow-running control is operated in a similar manner, i.e. moving to the right increases the speed of the engine and *vice versa*. (The slow-running control of the four-cylinder model is dealt with later.)

In front of the steering column is the windscreen wiper, and this is operated on the air-cooled model by moving the control lever to the left and then adjusting the regulating valve until the speed of the cleaning arm is suitable for the weather condition applying at the time. The farther the valve is opened the quicker will be the stroke of the cleaning arm. The water-cooled model (and some air-cooled models) employs an electric windscreen wiper, and this is set in motion by pulling the knurled knob out and giving it a twist, and is stopped by simply pressing in the knurled knob.

The remainder of the controls of the two models are on the instrument panel, and, as they differ somewhat, they will be dealt with separately.

Air-cooled Models. The dial on the extreme left is the speedometer and this indicates the speed at which you are travelling, and also the total mileage. To the right of the speedometer is the oil gauge which gives indication of the pressure of the oil being fed to the engine. The pressure should be between 2 lb. to 6 lb. when the engine is warm and the car is travelling at about 30 miles per hour.

Above the oil gauge is the instrument panel light and this is operated by turning the knob in a clockwise direction. On the right of the lamp is a somewhat smaller instrument, which is the ammeter. Its sensitive finger swings both to the right and to the left thus showing that the battery is being charged or discharged. When the lights are off and the dynamo and ignition switch is turned to the "winter" position, the ammeter needle should swing over to the right-hand side until it reads about 6 amp. when the car is running between 20 and 25 miles per hour. If the ammeter does not register when the dynamo and ignition switch is on, and the car is travelling at this speed, it means either that the fuse has blown, or that attention is necessary to the electrical system. (See Chapter VII.)

ON THE ROAD WITH THE THREE WHEELER 23

Below and to the right of the ammeter is a large black switch set in a circular dial. This controls the electrical circuits, serving the dual purpose of controlling the dynamo output and the lights.

FIG. 10. THE CONTROLS OF THE AIR-COOLED MODEL

KEY TO FIG. 10

A = Advance and retard lever
B = Slow-running control
C = Horn button
D = Dimming switch
E = Windscreen wiper (suction)
F = Carburettor strangler
G = Handbrake
H = Gear lever
I = Footbrake pedal
J = Accelerator pedal
K = Clutch pedal
L = Ignition, lighting, and charging switch
M = Starter button
N = Ammeter
O = Ignition warning light
P = Instrument panel light
Q = Oil gauge
R = Speedometer

There are four positions for this switch. When in the position in which the pointer head coincides with the words "Summer Half," it indicates that the dynamo is on half charge and only giving half its normal output. When the pointer coincides with the words "Winter Full," the dynamo is delivering its full output. When the pointer coincides with the words "Side," it means that the side and tail lamps are alight. When pointing to "Head," this means that the head, side, and tail lights are on. During the summer months the switch should be kept on the "Summer" mark, and during the winter on the "Winter" mark, as obviously the demand is then greater.

In the centre of the switch is a removable key. This serves to switch the ignition on and off. Turning the key clockwise switches on the ignition, turning it anti-clockwise switches off the ignition. If you remove the key when parking your car, put it in a safe place.

On the right of the switch will be found a projecting knob. This controls the strength of the mixture (that is, the amount of petrol in proportion to the amount of air) that is fed by the carburettor to the engine. When starting from cold, this knob should be pulled out as far as it will come, but on no account should the engine be run for any considerable time with the knob in this position. If this is done, neat petrol will be drawn into the cylinders. which will break down the oil film and may cause considerable damage. When the engine is firing evenly, this knob should be pressed inwards as far as it will go without causing the engine to spit or splutter. If the engine fails to run evenly with the mixture control knob pushed right in, it is probable that the engine is not warm enough.

Below and to the left of the mixture control knob is a projecting button. Pressure on this button has the result of turning the crankshaft of the engine, the same as is obtained by turning the starting handle. This button should be pressed firmly, and should be released immediately the engine fires.

To the left of this control is a red indicating light. When the dynamo output is insufficient to supply the needs of the ignition system the red light appears, indicating that current is being drawn for ignition purposes from the battery. Never leave the engine idling or stationary for long periods with this red light showing. If you do, it is quite likely that you will find your battery has been drained. Make a practice of switching the ignition off when the stop is to be of some duration.

Water-cooled Model. The dial on the extreme left is the speedometer. Above this dial is a projecting knurled knob. This is the slow-running control, which controls the speed of the engine when the foot is off the accelerator pedal. Turning it in an anti-clockwise direction increases the speed of the engine, while turning it in a clockwise direction has the opposite effect. It should be set so that the engine is just ticking over and then left in this position.

Next to this control is the instrument panel lamp and below it is the ammeter. To the right of the ammeter is the oil gauge, and the pressure reading should be about 60 lb. when the engine is warm and the car is travelling at about 30 miles per hour.

ON THE ROAD WITH THE THREE WHEELER 25

To the right of the oil gauge is the ignition and lighting switch. Below is the starter carburettor knob, and when the engine is cold it should be pulled out as far as it will come. *Do not depress*

FIG. 11. THE CONTROLS OF THE WATER-COOLED MODEL

A = Horn button
B = Dimming switch
C = Windscreen wiper (electric)
D = Handbrake lever
E = Footbrake pedal
F = Ignition, lighting and charging switch
G = Accelerator pedal
H = Gear lever
I = Starter control
J = Ammeter
K = Oil gauge
L = Ignition warning light
M = Footbrake pedal
N = Starter carburettor control
O = Instrument panel light
P = Speedometer
Q = Slow-running control

the accelerator pedal while this knob is out. When the engine is warm it will not be necessary to use this control.

To the left of this control is the ignition warning light, while still farther to the left is the self-starter, and this is operated by pulling the projecting knob out. Release this knob as soon as the engine fires.

Having mastered the controls we can now prepare the car for the road.

26   THE BOOK OF THE B.S.A. THREE WHEELER

Filling-up. First see that the radiator has sufficient water (rainwater is preferable), the correct level being within 1 in. of the filling orifice. Then make sure that there is sufficient petrol in the tank. Also see that the battery contains the correct quantity of acid and is properly charged (see Chapter VII), and that the tyres are inflated to the correct pressure (see page 107). The petrol tank, the filler cap for which is situated just under the rear of the bonnet, holds 4½ gal., 3¾ gal. being the main supply and ¾ gal. the reserve. Make sure that the engine, gearbox, clutch chamber, and differential case are supplied with the correct amount of oil (also the correct grade, see Chapter VI).

Starting-up. First see that the gear lever is in neutral, then turn on the petrol tap, which is in the centre of the car, above the pedal board. The handle will be in the closed position (pointing downwards) and turning to the right connects the main supply. Turning right over to the left brings in the reserve supply when the main supply is exhausted. Now set the ignition control lever which, as already stated, is in front of the steering wheel, in the fully retarded position (away from you). (As already stated, the four-cylinder model is fitted with automatic ignition advance and retard.)

The Twin-cylinder Model. Switch on the ignition by pressing in the key placed in the centre of the lighting switch on the instrument panel and turn it in a clockwise direction. As already stated, the engine starting switch is controlled by the button mounted on the instrument panel below the ammeter. When this switch is pressed the engine will be heard revolving and should start firing, when the button should be immediately released. In cold weather it is advisable to swing the engine by the starting handle with the ignition switched off before using the self-starter. It is bad practice to keep the starter button depressed if the engine is not revolving as sometimes happens if the battery is run down, or with a new stiff engine, or in very cold weather. Use the starter sparingly, and the battery will repay you by giving good, trouble-free service.

Occasionally it may be found necessary to use the starting handle to start the engine. A great point to remember when using the starting handle, is that the handle should be grasped by the right hand with the thumb on the same side of the handle as the fingers in order to avoid injury through the engine backfiring. (The correct hold is shown in Fig. 12.) Always pull the handle up with a sharp pull. It will be found much easier and less painful to use the handle if the rubber grip is removed and a piece of rag substituted in its place.

Four-cylinder Model. If the engine is cold, pull out the starter carburettor knob (the lower knob to the left on the instrument

ON THE ROAD WITH THE THREE WHEELER

panel) as far as it will come and pull the starter knob (on the right under the ammeter) firmly and decisively. The engine should start at once, and the self-starter knob should be released immediately, since the starter should not be left in action while the engine is running, or damage may be done. Then push in the starter carburettor knob, but if the engine spits back, pull it out again for a few moments until the engine runs steadily.

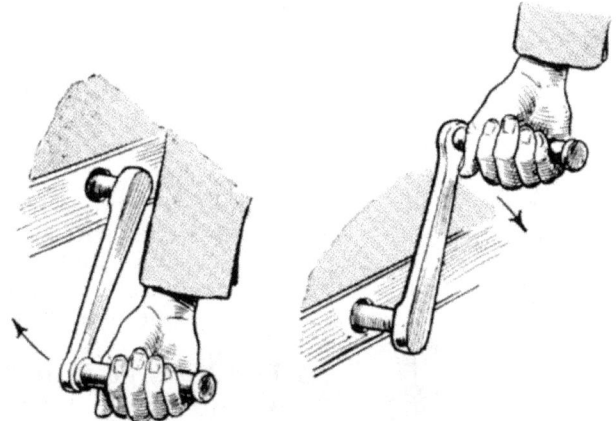

FIG. 12. CRANKING UP

Left: Correct method of using and gripping starting handle, viz. pulling up and gripping without thumb encircling handle.
Right: Incorrect method of using starting handle, viz. pushing down with thumb encircling handle.

Do not depress the accelerator pedal while this knob is out. When the engine is warm it is quite unnecessary to use this knob.

As already stated, to vary the speed at which the engine "ticks over" when the accelerator pedal is released a slow running control is fixed above the starter knob on the instrument panel. Turning this in the direction of the arrow marked on the knob has the effect of increasing the "tick over" speed.

Driving Off. (Both Models.) Having got the engine turning over slowly press the clutch pedal down (which is the left-hand pedal) and then engage low or first gear (to the left and backwards, see Fig. 13). Do not force the gear in; it should engage quite easily. Now release the handbrake (pull towards you), advance the ignition lever (air-cooled models), and let the clutch come up gradually; at the same time increase the speed of the engine by gently pressing the accelerator pedal. The car should now be moving smoothly away. The beginner will probably find that he either stops the engine or starts off with a jerk.

28 THE BOOK OF THE B.S.A. THREE WHEELER

This is caused by letting the clutch in too quickly, and should be rectified at an early stage, as enormous strains are placed upon the transmission.

After having travelled some few yards, the driver should attempt to change into second gear. (The road speed will be in the neighbourhood of 10 m.p.h.) To do this, again press the clutch pedal down, bring the gear lever into neutral position, then move the lever to the right and forward which will engage second speed gear. The change to top or third is more simple and should be made fairly quickly. Put out the clutch and pull the gear lever straight back towards you and then release the clutch. You are now in top and doing famously, but don't take any liberties yet.

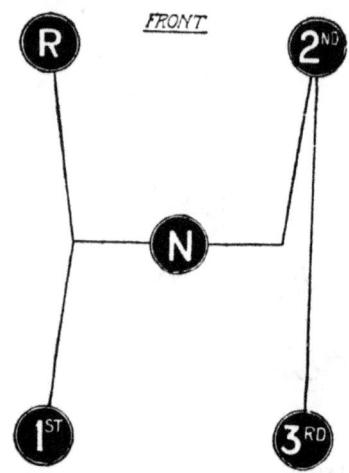

Fig. 13. Showing the Gear Positions

Reverse gear is obtained by putting out the clutch, and moving the gear lever (from neutral) to the left and forward.

A Few Hints on Gear Changing.

If you have bungled the gear change, and cannot get into the desired position, don't lose your temper and try to force the lever into position. Stop the car by pressing the left and right pedals, put the gear lever back into the neutral position, and start from the beginning. Not only will this save the gears from being damaged, it will also give you additional practice. Remember the old saying: "Practice Makes Perfect," and you will realize you are not wasting time.

Never try to engage a "forward" speed while travelling backwards or, *vice versa*, reverse while travelling forwards. Always make certain the car is stationary before engaging a gear which will reverse the direction of travel.

When changing to a higher gear the left (clutch) pedal must always be pushed right down and the foot removed from the middle (accelerator) pedal until the change has been made. A slight pause in the neutral position may be advisable when the engine is hot.

When changing down to a lower gear, the clutch pedal should only be lightly depressed, and after waiting for approximately half a second with the right foot pressing on the middle (accelerator) pedal, so that the engine can gain speed, the change can be made. Double-declutching (practised by all "old hands") is the

ON THE ROAD WITH THE THREE WHEELER   29

best method for changing down, and is, in fact, the only correct way to ensure a quiet and easy change to a lower gear.

(The beginner should not attempt this, however, but must wait until he has had a certain amount of "straight" gear changing.) The procedure is as follows—

Holding the gear lever lightly, push down the clutch pedal, move the gear lever into neutral position, and let the clutch pedal rise again. Now "rev" the engine up by pressing the accelerator pedal, put the clutch out and move the gear lever smartly into the required position, once more taking your foot off the clutch pedal. After a time this will become "second nature" to you, and all downward changes will be positive. A great point to remember is that you should never look down when changing gear.

CARE OF THE CAR

Running-in New Engines. After buying a brand new B.S.A., special caution must be exercised for a certain period of driving, in order to allow all moving parts to become bedded down and bearing surfaces to harden. Any attempt to expedite matters is doomed to failure and may permanently spoil the engine. Until 500 miles have been covered, a speed in excess of 30 m.p.h. in top gear should not be attained, and large throttle openings should not be used.

New engines should be given frequent attention during the first 500 miles if they are to give long and trouble-free service. After the first 250 miles the tappet clearances should be checked and adjusted if necessary (see pages 35 and 48). The cylinder head stud nuts (water-cooled models) should also have attention at the same time. The oil should be drained and the engine refilled with fresh oil (see page 86) after the first 500 miles have been covered: the oil filter should be thoroughly cleaned at the same time.

Use of the Ignition Lever. As has been mentioned previously, a hand control is provided on the air-cooled models for the purpose of advancing or retarding the ignition at will. Intelligent use should be made of this lever, particularly if the driver expects the engine to accelerate from a low speed on top gear; in such circumstances the control lever should be moved to the retard position and gradually advanced as the engine speed increases. As already stated, the water-cooled models are provided with automatic advance and retard controlled by a governor forming part of the distributor assembly. As the engine speed increases the governor advances the ignition which retards with falling engine revolutions.

When the car is travelling at a reasonable road speed, say

of above fifteen to eighteen miles per hour, the ignition should be kept in the fully-advanced position. The retarding of the ignition for hill climbing is hardly good practice, as if the engine is showing signs of distress a gear change to a lower ratio is indicated as being overdue. Careful use of the ignition control must not be confused with its use as a means to careless driving with no consideration for the engine.

Use of the Brakes. It is the fault of many drivers to "drive on the brakes," that is, to apply the brakes vigorously and often in a somewhat erratic manner. This is very bad practice, as not only are the brake linings quickly worn away in consequence, but also the life of the tyres and the transmission system generally is considerably shortened.

The expert allows the engine to act as a brake, when a gentler retardation is effected and skidding risks minimized.

A change to second gear when approaching a severe bend will slow the car appreciably, so that a violent application of the footbrake is rendered unnecessary.

Likewise the descent of lengthy and severe gradients should be made on a lower gear, and if second or first gear is used it is often possible to descend an extremely severe hill without even touching the brakes. This practice is not detrimental to the engine in any way.

During the autumn and winter weather, the roads are often exceedingly treacherous, due either to decaying leaves on the surface or to greasiness, resultant of morning frost and mist. At such times especially, violent application of the brakes should be avoided, thus neutralizing as far as possible the probability of a skid.

To change from top to second on a B.S.A. is extremely simple, and if the driver is approaching a bend of any severity, it is an easy matter to engage the lower ratio before the bend is reached. One can then accelerate round the bend, a definitely safer method than rounding it on the over-run. Moreover, one has at one's command the extra engine power for either increased speed or retardation essential for coping with emergencies. Negotiated in this manner, the corner is taken with an absolute minimum of risk.

Furthermore, all braking should be carried out as far as possible when the car is travelling in a straight line, the possibility of a skid being reduced if this is done.

Care of the Wings. The wings are stove-enamelled and should not be rubbed with a dry duster, as this is likely to scratch the enamel. Always wash them down with a soft sponge or hose, using plenty of water. On no account attempt to remove tar spots with the aid of paraffin or petrol. There are a number of special preparations on the market which remove tar spots without harming the enamel.

After the wings have been well washed down with hose and sponge, all beads of water remaining should be carefully cleaned off with a chamois leather.

Chromium Plating. It should be noted that chromium plating does not require, and should not be treated with, metal polish, for it does not oxidize in the same manner as nickel-plating. The chromium-plated parts should be treated in the same way as the wings, and the surfaces will then improve with cleaning.

CHAPTER V

MAINTENANCE AND OVERHAUL

IN this chapter the author has endeavoured to provide in a readily accessible form just that information which B.S.A. three-wheeler owners require in order to keep their cars in good mechanical order and tune. Little skill or bother is required to maintain in first-class condition any of the B.S.A. engines, and no assistance is needed when decarbonizing or carrying out adjustments.

Periodical attention in the way of adjustments and regular decarbonizing and valve grinding well repays the owner as it keeps performance up to scratch. Incidentally, it may be mentioned here that the wise driver will occasionally go over all the nuts on his car with a spanner to see that they are kept tight, and will systematically and regularly inspect the mechanism to ensure that everything is as it should be. A loose nut which may appear to be of trivial importance if neglected may lead to considerable trouble and expense.

It is proposed to deal with the popular 90-degree, V-twin, overhead-valve, air-cooled engine first, and then to deal with the more recently designed monobloc four-cylinder water-cooled engine. Coil ignition maintenance and lubrication are dealt with elsewhere and will *not* be referred to here, the concluding paragraphs of this chapter being devoted to miscellaneous chassis adjustments and dismantling operations, and also carburettor maintenance and the detection of engine trouble.

AIR-COOLED O.H.V. ENGINES

Keep the Plugs Clean. Freedom from misfiring, easy starting, good slow running and a full power output are all dependent to a very great extent on the sparking plugs, which require regular attention if engine efficiency is to be maintained. This attention which consists of keeping the electrodes clean and the gaps correctly adjusted, is particularly important during the early period of an engine's life, because until the piston rings and cylinder bore attain a uniform glass-like surface and fit each other perfectly, a considerable amount of oil finds its way into the combustion chambers and fouls the plugs from time to time. Another point the author would emphasize is that it is false economy to use poor quality plugs. Apart from causing a lot of unnecessary bother they also tend to increase the fuel consumption. The plug

MAINTENANCE AND OVERHAUL

recommended for use on B.S.A. O.H.V. Three Wheelers is the Lodge C3. This type gives excellent results.

To clean a Lodge C3 plug thoroughly it should be taken to pieces. In order to do this it is best to employ a box spanner on

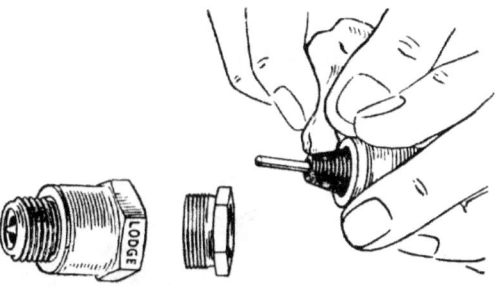

FIG. 14. CLEAN PLUG INSULATION WITH A PETROL-SOAKED RAG

the gland nut, as this eliminates the risk of distorting the metal case. Should a vice be used to hold the plug while unscrewing the gland nut, be careful not to tighten the vice so as to clamp it. It is quite sufficient to close up the vice jaws so that the plug is merely prevented from rotating. Having dismantled the plug, clean the insulation with a rag soaked in petrol (see Fig. 14), but do not scrape it unless the carbon deposits are very difficult to remove, or defective insulation may be caused. Examine the insulation for any signs of cracking which sometimes is caused through overheating. Metal parts of the plug can, of course, be cleaned with paraffin or can be scraped (Fig. 15), as these are not liable to damage like the insulation. If the plugs are sooted this indicates an over rich mixture.

Before reassembling the plug, clean up the electrode points with a piece of smooth emery paper and also make sure that no grit has lodged in the joint between the body of the plug and the insulator. This is important, otherwise gas leakage may occur. Finally, after assembly adjust the spark gap to ·030 in. by bending the earth or side electrodes.

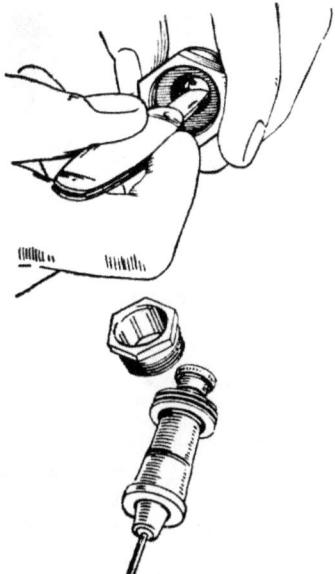

FIG. 15. CARBON MAY BE SCRAPED OFF METAL PARTS WITH A POCKET KNIFE

34 THE BOOK OF THE B.S.A. THREE WHEELER

Use a feeler gauge to measure the gap. Suitable gauges may be obtained from Messrs. Lodge Plugs, Ltd., of Rugby, free of charge, provided 1½d. is enclosed to cover postage. When replacing the plugs in the cylinders see that the copper washers are also replaced, and if the compression sealing washers are at all damaged, fit new ones.

Keep an Eye on the Contact-breaker. Occasionally the distributor moulding should be removed and the contact-breaker (Fig. 16) examined. The contacts C must be kept absolutely

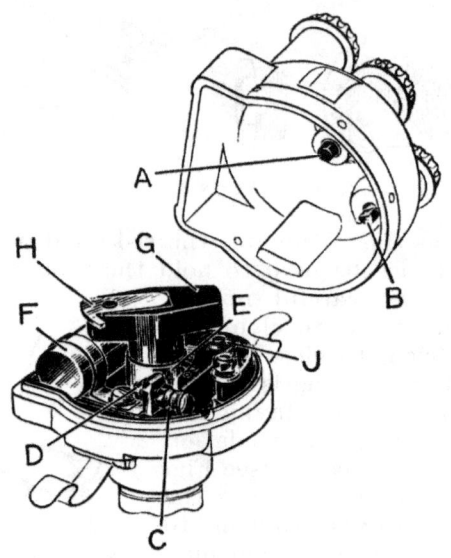

FIG. 16. THE DISTRIBUTOR AND CONTACT-BREAKER

(On the four-cylinder models the device is similar except that there are two extra terminals.)

A = Carbon brush
B = Electrodes
C = Contacts
D = Locking nut
E = Rotating cam
F = Condenser
G = Rotatory distributor arm
H = Metal electrodes
J = Contact-breaker pivot

free from oil or grease, and if at all burned the contacts should be cleaned with very fine emery cloth and afterwards wiped with a petrol-soaked rag. Dirty contacts are liable to cause a lot of trouble which can easily be avoided. In the unlikely event of the points being pitted it may be necessary to true up the contacts with a very fine file. This is a delicate operation, and only the barest amount of metal must be removed.

Examine the gap between the contacts when fully open, and if this exceeds ·004 in.–·006 in., it shows that the fibre heel has worn and the fixed contact requires adjusting. To do this, rotate

MAINTENANCE AND OVERHAUL 35

the engine until the contacts are wide open, and then slacken with the ignition spanner the locknut D and rotate the fixed contact screw by its hexagon head until the contact-breaker gap is correctly adjusted. Afterwards, be sure to retighten the locknut. Frequent contact-breaker adjustment is not advised. It may be observed that the form of the two contact-breaker cams is different. The longer cam applies to the nearside cylinder.

Besides keeping the contacts clean it is important also to keep the distributor electrodes clean and free of deposits.

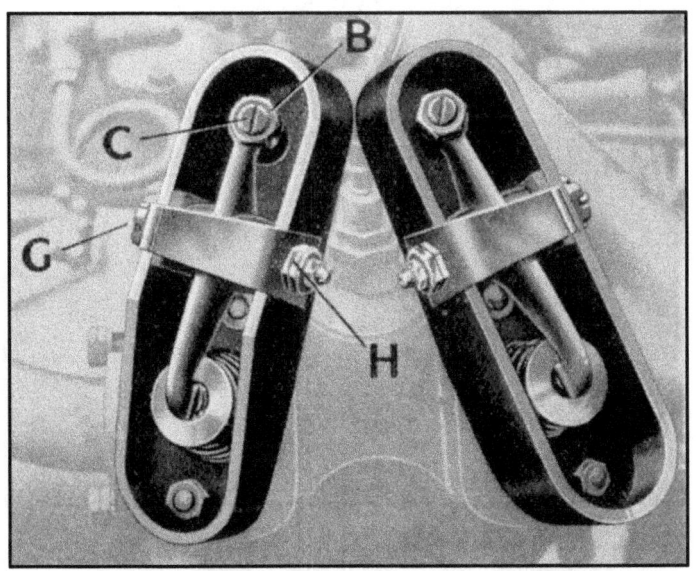

Fig. 17. Illustrating the Overhead Valve Gear and Means of Adjustment

Tappet Adjustment. Owing to the very robust construction and generous dimensions of the overhead valve gear and the adequate provision made for lubricating the overhead rockers, it should not be necessary to adjust the tappets except at very infrequent intervals, but the clearances between the ends of the rocker arms and the valve stems should be checked immediately there is any suggestion of the engine losing its sweetness or becoming noisy. It is most important to keep these clearances correct, otherwise the valve timing is affected to some extent and the valve lift also, which markedly affects the performance of a high-speed engine, resulting in poor slow running and uneven pulling, together with a considerable reduction in power output.

Further, the valves, and particularly the exhaust valves, are liable to suffer injury due to overheating.

In order to check the valve clearances with a feeler gauge, remove the rocker box covers of the cylinder receiving attention by releasing the spring clips (see Fig. 18) holding them in place, and by means of the starting handle slowly rotate the engine until the inlet valve has just closed, and then give the handle

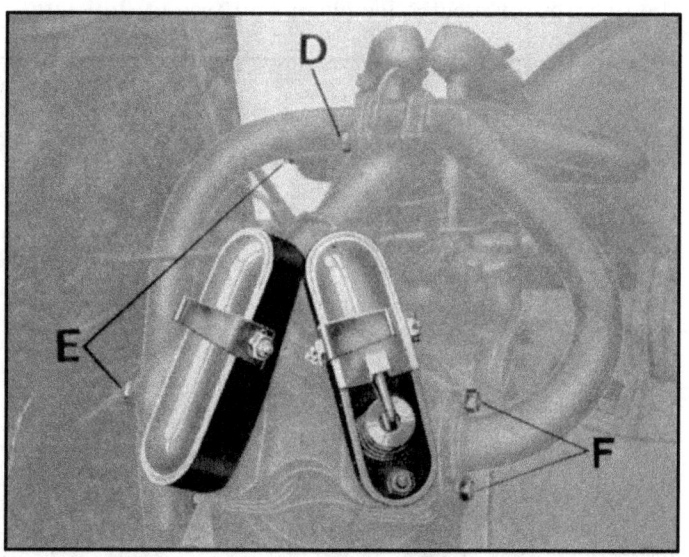

Fig. 18. Points to be Looked to Prior to Cylinder Removal

another quarter of a turn. This will bring the piston to the top of the compression stroke when both valves are, of course, fully closed. It will greatly facilitate matters if the sparking plug is removed so as to prevent compression in the cylinder. Now insert a feeler gauge of $1\frac{1}{2}$ thousandths of an inch (·0015 in.) between the rocker arm and valve stem. It should just go in without binding *when the engine is cold*. This adjustment is correct for both inlet and exhaust valves.

On no account should the tappets be adjusted except when the engine is *stone* cold, otherwise the valves may be damaged. This is most important. To adjust the tappets, first slacken off the hexagon locking nut *B* (Fig. 17) and then adjust the screw *C* up or down as required with a screwdriver. Finally, securely retighten the locking nut.

Before dealing with the second cylinder be sure to put the piston on T.D.C. on the compression stroke, and it is best not to make irregular adjustments, i.e. attending to one tappet one day and another later on, but to check and adjust them all at the same time.

When to Decarbonize. It is impossible to lay down a hard and fast rule as to the mileage that should be covered before

FIG. 19. SHOWING HOW THE CYLINDERS CAN BE REMOVED WITHOUT DISTURBING THE INDUCTION, EXHAUST MANIFOLDS, OR OIL PIPES

it becomes necessary to remove the cylinders and scrape out the carbon deposits (due to burnt oil, road dust, and products of combustion) from inside the cylinder heads and from the piston crowns. Generally speaking, however, it should not be necessary to "decoke" more often than *once every* 5,000 *miles*. Much depends on how the machine is driven and looked after. But immediately the engine becomes at all "rough" and displays a tendency to knock under ordinary running conditions and to lose its power, it may be presumed that decarbonizing is necessary to restore engine efficiency. It may be mentioned that the more thoroughly an engine is decarbonized the longer will it be before this operation is again required.

Decarbonizing and valve grinding are perfectly simple, and one person should have no difficulty in tackling the task unaided if he goes the right way about it.

How to Remove the Cylinders. Although it is not essential to remove the bonnet when decarbonizing, it is advisable to do so because, with the bonnet out of the way, the engine is naturally much more accessible and easy to work upon. Take out the two sparking plugs and then slacken off the nuts on bolts *D* (Fig. 18) until it is just possible to free the joint washers. Having done this, the two set pins *E* on each cylinder should be unscrewed and removed and the two exhaust union nuts *F* should be slackened. Next disconnect the oil pipes and swing them clear. To do this, unscrew the two oil pipe nipples at the base of each cylinder and slacken off the nuts at the other ends of the pipe (i.e. at the "Y" union on the oil control body). The cylinders can now be drawn off as soon as the cylinder flange nuts have been removed.

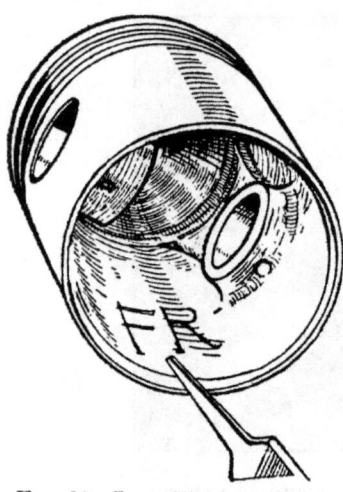

Fig. 20. It is Wise to Mark Each Piston After Removal

Each cylinder should be held firmly with both hands while drawing it off, and special care should be taken to avoid putting any strain on the piston or connecting-rod. As the piston emerges from the mouth of the cylinder be most careful not to let the skirt of the piston strike the crankcase or connecting-rod sharply (see Fig. 19), as this is extremely likely to cause distortion, possibly not apparent to the eye, of the piston or even to crack it. Aluminium alloy pistons are very accurately made and very fragile. For this reason, as soon as a cylinder has been taken off a rag should be wrapped around each connecting-rod. Doing this also eliminates the considerable danger of foreign bodies entering the crankcase. Better still, take off both pistons.

To Remove the Pistons. It is only necessary to push out with the fingers the fully-floating gudgeon-pins which are sliding fits in the pistons and have soft metal end caps to prevent scoring of the cylinder walls. It is very important indeed not to interchange the pistons and to replace them exactly as they were before removal. To ensure this being done, it is a wise plan to mark the inside of each piston as shown in Fig. 20, where the letters "FR" have been scratched with a file to indicate that this is the front side of the right-hand (i.e. off-side) piston.

Valve Removal. Having removed the cylinders and pistons, the next thing to do before proceeding with decarbonizing is the removal of the valves from the cylinder heads. This permits of all the carbon deposits inside the cylinder heads being scraped off and the valves being inspected and, if necessary, ground-in. To remove the valves, proceed as follows.

Remove the rocker-box covers and nuts *G* (Fig. 17) which hold the rocker pins in position and tap out the pins *H*. Each rocker can then be lifted out. Now take the valve spring compressor tool included in the tool kit and substitute it for one of

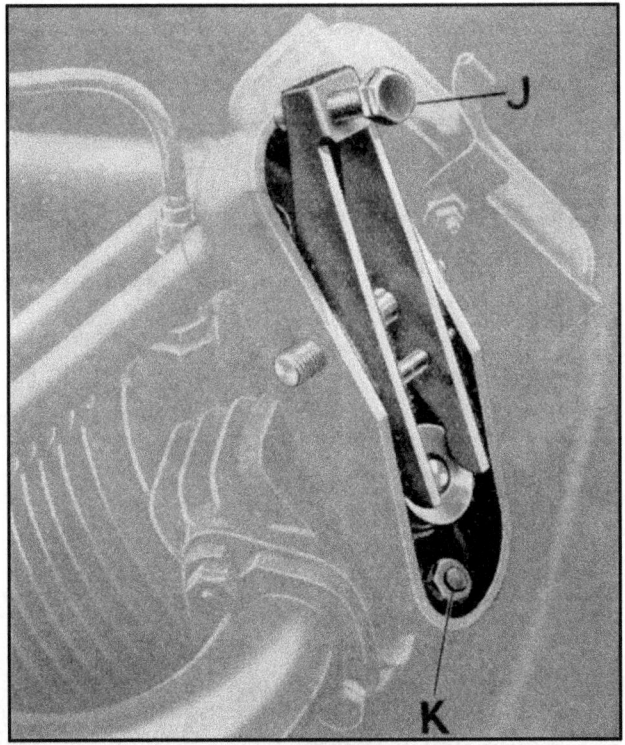

Fig. 21. How to Use the B.S.A. Valve Spring Compressor

the rockers, inserting the rocker pin *H* to retain it in position as shown in Fig. 21. In the tool kit is a tommy-bar for use with the various box spanners. Insert this tommy-bar through the sparking plug hole until its end bears against the head of the valve inside the cylinder. Then press down on the outer end of the tommy-bar and at the same time rotate the screw *J* clockwise with a spanner until the two halves of the split collet securing the valve spring can be removed with the fingers. If they are inclined to stick, give a sharp tap on the valve spring collar which should free them. Remove the tommy-bar and the compressor, withdraw the valve spring and its collar, and also the little spring

ring on the valve stem, when the valve can be withdrawn downwards into the cylinder barrel. Deal similarly with the other three valves and be careful not to mix them up. To remove the rocker-boxes, undo the two nuts K which retain each box on the cylinder head.

Decarbonizing. All carbon deposits can now be carefully scraped off the inside of the cylinder heads. For this purpose a fairly blunt screwdriver will be found as good as anything,

Fig. 22. Do Not Overlook Carbon Deposits Inside Each Piston

although special decarbonizing scrapers are obtainable. Do not scratch the combustion chamber walls unnecessarily because in practice it is found that a rough surface carbonizes considerably more quickly than does a smooth one. Chip off all carbon deposits in the neighbourhood of the exhaust ports where deposits are usually found to be heavy, and also in the case of engines having had considerable usage, just above the point in each cylinder where the piston completes its stroke. Here a slight ridge to which carbon clings very readily is often found. When removing the carbon avoid touching the polished cylinder bore. Finally, when all traces of carbon have been removed, rinse each cylinder out with a little paraffin and then wipe the whole of the interior with a clean oily rag, making sure that every trace of carbon particles has been removed.

In the case of aluminium alloy pistons, the carbon cannot be removed by any method such as the immersion of the piston in a caustic soda solution, as this attacks the alloy and there is no alternative but to carefully scrape all deposits off the piston crowns, using for this purpose a rather blunt penknife or other implement such as a wood chisel or a screwdriver. Here, again, be careful not to scratch deeply the comparatively soft aluminium alloy surfaces. The use of emery cloth is not advised as it is very difficult to remove subsequently all traces of abrasive particles which tend to become embedded and later may cause

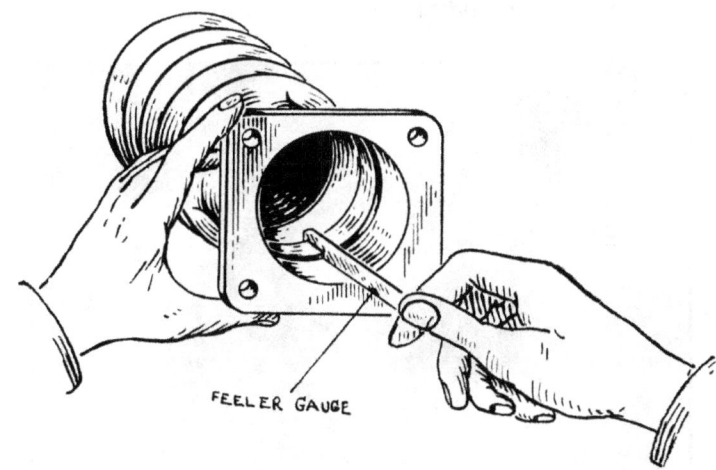

FIG. 23. HOW TO TEST THE GAP AT A PISTON RING SLOT

considerable mischief. If final polishing is desired, the best course is to clean the piston crowns with a paraffin-soaked rag and then use fine quality metal polish. Polishing is, of course, not essential, but some owners consider this refinement worth while. Do not touch the sides of the pistons, except in the case of the lands between the top rings and the crowns. Whatever carbon deposits are found here should be removed. If the carbon deposits found here on the outside of the pistons are heavy, it is possible that there are also deposits *inside* the pistons caused by burnt lubricating oil. Remove the whole of this.

Examining and Removing Piston Rings. Since the rings are the mainstay of engine compression, their condition is vitally important, and when decarbonizing they should always be examined and if necessary removed. Should the rings be quite free in their grooves and bright all over, do not disturb them. If, however, they are at all gummed up, they should be removed and the grooves carefully cleaned. All carbon deposits should also be removed from the backs of the rings and also from the ends forming the gaps. Carbon deposits here, if slight, may be beneficial as they increase the compression seal, but if heavy, often they tend to cause partial engine seizure when the engine gets hot owing to the fact that piston ring expansion is not counteracted by the rings closing in. Should any ring show brown patches on its working face, it has probably become worn, distorted, or has lost its springiness, and should at once be removed and replaced by a new ring.

A word here about piston ring gaps. The correct gap is ·015 in., and on no account should the gap err to any extent on the small

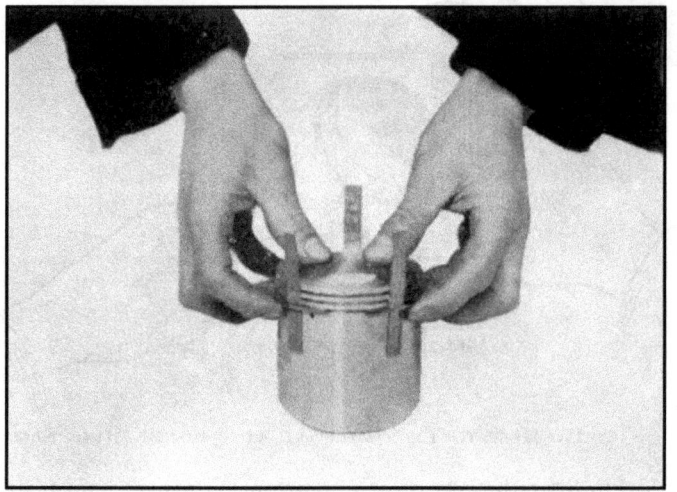

FIG. 24. HOW TO REMOVE PISTON RINGS SAFELY

side from this figure. A larger gap if not excessive will not cause any trouble other than slightly weakened compression, but it is definitely time to renew a ring if the gap is greater than ·025 in. Fig. 23 shows how to test for correct piston ring gap. The ring being tested should be inserted in the cylinder a few inches and pushed square with the piston. The measurement at the gap can then be ascertained by means of a feeler gauge as shown.

Piston rings, it should be mentioned, are made of cast iron, and, owing to their method of manufacture and heat treatment, are exceedingly brittle. They cannot be safely sprung out wider than the piston crown diameter, and careless handling invariably results in fracture. The only really safe method of removing them is to use a special removal tool (an inexpensive tool called the "Brico" is made by the British Chuck and Piston Ring Co.), or else to employ the popular method shown in Fig. 24. Three strips of sheet tin about 1½ in. long and ⅜ in. wide are inserted

MAINTENANCE AND OVERHAUL

under the rings opposite the gaps, enabling the rings to be eased off one by one. Broken pieces of an old hacksaw blade answer the same purpose and are perhaps preferable, as they are less liable to injure the grooves or the lands between them. Piston rings which are badly gummed up cannot usually be removed without breakage, but if they are not stuck very firmly it is

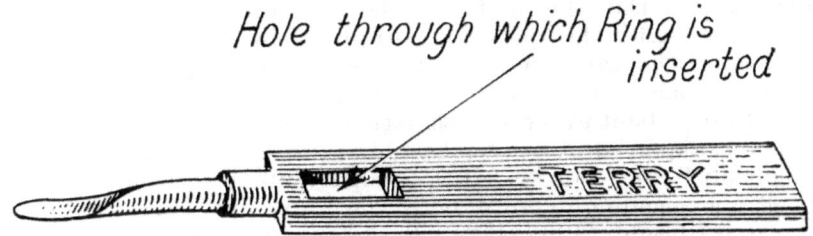

FIG. 25. AN EXCELLENT TOOL FOR REMOVING STUCK PISTON RINGS

generally possible to remove them by allowing the piston to soak in a paraffin bath, and then to ease off the rings with a suitable tool such as that shown in Fig. 25, which is strongly recommended.

Grinding-in the Valves. Engine compression and engine efficiency depend to a very great extent upon the state of the valves

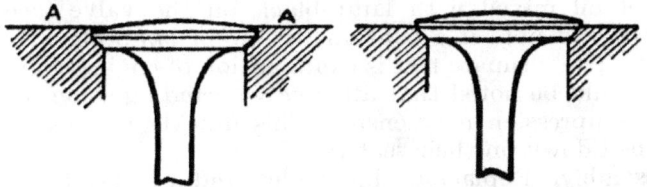

FIG. 26. WHAT EXCESSIVE GRINDING-IN DOES
The valve shown at AA has become pocketed.

which, when closed, must prevent gas leakage at high explosion pressures. Thus, whenever decarbonizing is undertaken, the valves should be examined and ground-in if necessary. It is not always necessary to grind-in the valves when decarbonizing, but this should be done if an inspection reveals that the valve faces and/or seats are at all pitted. Should the pit marks on the valves be at all deep (which is sometimes found after a big mileage has been covered), grinding-in should not be attempted, as the amount of grinding-in necessary to restore the valves to good condition will almost certainly result in the valves becoming "pocketed" as shown in Fig. 26, and this interferes with induction efficiency (gas velocity is about 180 ft. per sec.), and produces loss of power. Instead, the valves should be dispatched to the B.S.A. works at Small Heath, Birmingham, in order to be refaced.

To grind-in a *slightly* pitted valve, proceed as follows: Clean the valve first, and then smear a thin film of fine grade grinding paste (such as Richford's), or flour of emery mixed with engine oil, around the valve face. Now insert the valve in its guide, making sure that the right valve is used, and grip the end of the valve stem with the special tool supplied in the B.S.A. tool kit. Then pull the valve up against its seat and rotate it about half a turn in one direction, and then an equal amount in the opposite direction. About every six oscillations lower the valve and rotate it about a quarter of a revolution, and proceed as before, stopping when no "cut" can be felt to redistribute the grinding paste. Continue grinding-in until both the valve face and valve seat are quite bright. Line contact is not really enough, but beware of excessive valve grinding for the reason already mentioned. On the completion of valve grinding *be most careful to remove all traces of grinding compound* from both the valves and cylinder head. Finally, if the valve stems are dirty or rough, polish with fine emery cloth. Some enthusiasts finish off by polishing the valves with metal polish, but this is really a refinement of doubtful value except for high-speed racing, when gas "skin friction" is quite an important factor.

Testing Valves After Grinding-in. A good method is to smear a film of oil mixed with lamp-black on the valve face, insert the valve and note if a continuous line of lamp-black is left on the seat. The ultimate test is examination of engine compression, but it should be noted that after valve grinding some temporary loss of compression may ensue. This quickly disappears as the valves bed down on their seats.

Reassembly. Replacing the valves and overhead valve gear is simply a reversal of the dismantling operations, but there are two important points to which attention is directed. In the first place, do not forget to replace the small spring ring in the groove on each valve stem. Secondly, when replacing the rockers be absolutely sure that the rocker pin nuts G (Fig. 17) are perfectly tight.

Having replaced the four valves and refitted the rocker-boxes, carefully wipe each piston clean and replace it in the correct position on its connecting-rod, taking care not to interchange either the pistons or the gudgeon-pins. Each cylinder may now be refitted after first smearing the walls of the piston and cylinder with some clean engine oil, taking care that the push-rod tubes and push-rods are correctly positioned and that the soft washers which make an oil-tight joint at the upper and lower ends of the tubes are still in place. Having replaced the cylinders and overhead valve gear it only remains to reconnect the manifolds and

MAINTENANCE AND OVERHAUL

the oil pipes in the reverse order to that given for dismantling. Finally check and, if necessary, adjust the valve clearances and refit the rocker-box covers. The engine is now ready for starting, but note that on the assumption that the valves have been ground-in it may be necessary to readjust the tappets again after a mileage of about 50 has been covered, because the valves take some time to bed down thoroughly on their seats during which, of course, the tappet clearances become smaller than originally set.

Do Not Interfere With the Relief Valve. On the B.S.A. engines a relief or by-pass valve (see Figs. 46 and 47) is incorporated

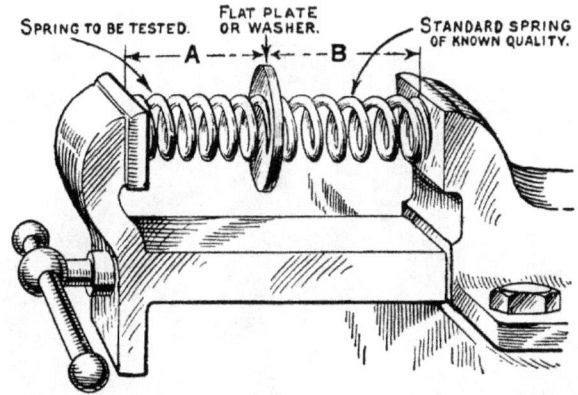

FIG. 27. A SIMPLE METHOD OF TESTING A VALVE SPRING

in the main vertical oil passage above the oil pump with the object of ensuring an adequate oil supply at moderate cruising speeds, and, at the same time, a supply which is not excessive at large throttle openings. The valve is of simple construction. It comprises a ball held against its seating by a compression spring. When the engine is revving fast, the oil pressure is sufficient to raise the ball off its seating and permit of some of the oil passing directly into the timing case, while when the engine is revving slowly the ball is held in contact with its seating and the whole of the oil has to pass up the vertical pipe D (Fig. 46). Interference with the tension of the spring in the relief valve is strongly deprecated, and may cause serious trouble. It should be mentioned that the spring tension is carefully adjusted on all B.S.A. engines before the cars are dispatched from the works.

Fitting New Valve Springs. After very considerable use, valve springs are apt to lose their compression strength somewhat, and in some cases may actually break. It is a simple matter, however, to fit new springs at any time should this be necessary, using the special valve spring compressor supplied in the tool kit and already referred to on page 38. When fitting a new valve spring, make quite sure that the split collet halves bed down properly in the groove on the valve stem. It is quite impossible for a valve to drop down into the cylinder when its spring is removed, *provided the safety spring ring just below the collet groove*

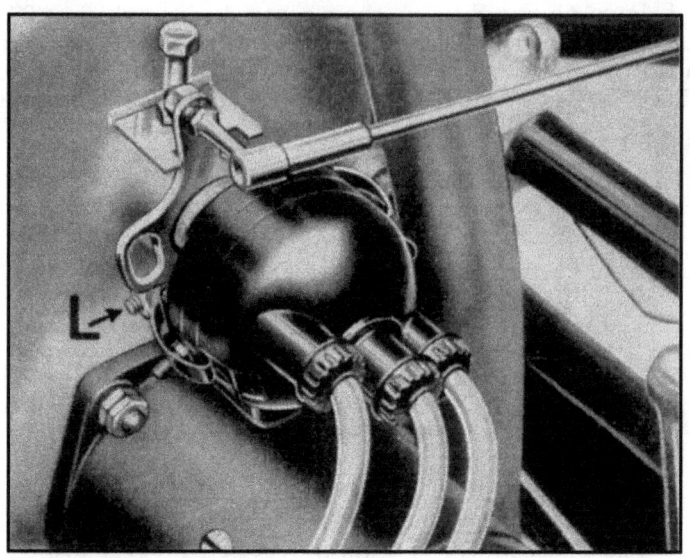

Fig. 28. Showing Location of Distributor Fixing Nut

is in position. It is, therefore, most important to see that this ring is not accidentally removed while the cylinders are in place.

A good and simple method of testing a valve spring is illustrated in Fig. 27. A new spring of known quality and strength is placed, with a washer interposed, end on to the spring being tested, and the two springs are gripped between the jaws of a vice. On tightening up the vice, the distance A may be found to be shorter than the distance B. If this is the case, clearly the valve spring has lost its original strength and requires replacement.

Wash Out Exhaust Rocker-boxes Every 1,000 Miles. Congealed or carbonized oil tends to collect in the neighbourhood of the exhaust valves and springs, and it is therefore advisable about once every 1,000 miles to remove the exhaust rocker-box covers and wash out the rocker-boxes with some petrol or paraffin. Removal of the exhaust valves does, of course, enable the job to be done more thoroughly than is possible with the valves in place.

MAINTENANCE AND OVERHAUL 47

How to Check and Set the Ignition Timing. In order to check the ignition timing which must be correct to obtain maximum efficiency, fully retard the ignition lever which is situated on front of the steering column. Now rotate the engine with the starting handle (removal of the plugs will facilitate this) until the inlet valve on the near side (i.e. the left side) cylinder has just closed. Then, after removing the filling plug from the top of the fly-wheel pit, rotate the engine farther until the mark "TCI" on the fly-wheel rim comes in line with the centre of the hole, taking a sight from the rear. The piston in the near-side cylinder will then be on the top dead centre (T.D.C.) position on the compression stroke in which position the spark must be timed to occur. To do this, take off the cover of the distributor and slacken the nut L (Fig. 28). The body of the distributor can then be rotated clockwise or anti-clockwise until the contacts C (Fig. 16) of the contact-breaker show a feeler gauge clearance of ·004 in. to ·006 in. Finally retighten nut L and make certain that the maximum opening of the contacts lies between ·012 in. and ·015 in. The engine is now correctly timed, and the distributor body cover may be replaced. In certain cases, according to the fuel used and special road conditions, it may be advisable to use an ignition advance greater than the normal setting just described.

WATER-COOLED S.V. ENGINE

Cleaning Non-detachable Plugs. The sparking plugs recommended and fitted on the B.S.A. S.V. models are Lodge S14. They are 14 m.m. plugs, or what are commonly referred to as "baby" plugs. During

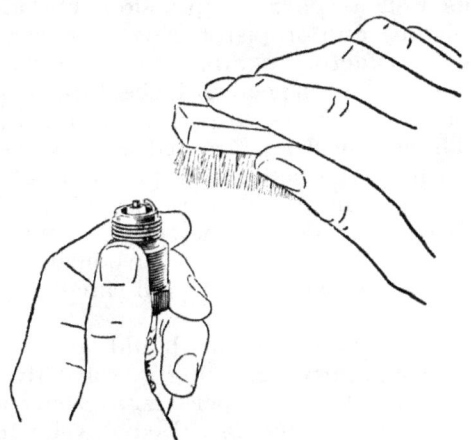

FIG. 29. HOW TO CLEAN NON-DETACHABLE PLUGS

an engine's "teething" stages, or running-in period, rather frequent cleaning of the plugs is necessary, and, of course, throughout the life of a plug the gap at the electrodes should be regularly examined and, if necessary, adjusted by bending the earth or side electrodes towards the centre pin. Under the influence of terrific combustion chamber heat, the gaps at the plug electrodes tend to gradually widen. Apart from causing inefficiency with possibly excessive fuel consumption and difficult starting, too large plug gaps throw an undue strain upon the coil. The gaps should be set and maintained at ·018 in. As mentioned on page 34, a suitable gauge is obtainable free from the plug manufacturers.

The Lodge 14 m.m. plugs are of the non-detachable type, and therefore cannot be cleaned by detaching the centre insulated electrode. To clean plugs of this type the best plan is to remove the carbon deposits from the electrode points with a stiff wire brush (see Fig. 29).

The Contact Breaker. Keep this clean and correctly adjusted. The instructions given on page 34 are applicable to the contact breaker on the four-cylinder engine.

Tappet Adjustment. For reasons already mentioned on page 35, tappet clearances must be maintained correct. On the water-cooled, four-cylinder, side-valve engine, incorrect clearances besides resulting in loss of power, considerable clicking noise and possibly poor compression and a change in the exhaust note, may also cause considerable overheating and perhaps boiling of the water in the radiator.

Insufficient tappet clearances often lead to burnt exhaust valves as well as poor compression, but always remember that faulty pistons and/or piston rings can also be responsible for absence of satisfactory compression on using the starting handle. These should be suspected if the tappet clearances are found correct and the valves are in good condition. However, if a B.S.A. Three Wheeler is treated with respect during that vital part of its life—the running-in period (see page 29), and the oil in the sump is maintained at the proper level, the piston rings and pistons should give no trouble for thousands of miles, other than the possible need for decarbonizing the grooves (dealt with in a preceding paragraph) from time to time. Even this is very rarely necessary.

Tappet adjustment should always be checked and, if necessary, adjusted after grinding-in the valves. They should also be inspected at regular periods, say once a month, whether the symptoms previously described develop or not, and *always with the engine stone cold.*

To check the clearances, proceed as follows: Expose the tappet heads by unscrewing the pair of knurled nuts A (Fig. 30) on the left-hand side of the engine and removing the cover plate B. Now, *with the ignition switched off,* insert the starting handle and rotate the engine until No. 2 tappet (see Fig. 31) has ascended to the highest position. Then take from the tool kit the feeler gauge and find out whether the ·006 in. blade will just pass between the tappet head C of No. 1 tappet and the (exhaust) valve stem D. If it fails to enter or enters with room to spare, adjust the clearance by holding the tappet head nut C with one spanner and with

MAINTENANCE AND OVERHAUL

another unlock nut *E* by turning clockwise, afterwards screwing the tappet head *C* up or down as required. Having made the necessary adjustment, lock nut *E* by holding the tappet head and turning the locknut clockwise. See that it is firmly locked, but do not use a hammer for this purpose. Finally check the tappet clearance once again. The clearance for No. 2 (inlet)

FIG. 30. NEAR-SIDE GENERAL VIEW OF FOUR-CYLINDER POWER UNIT
(It should be noted that a fuel pump is *not* fitted to the Four-cylinder Three Wheeler.)

tappet should be ·004 in., and is set in the same way. The other exhaust and inlet tappets, Nos. 4, 5, and 8, and Nos. 3, 6, and 7, are similarly adjusted.

To check No. 2 tappet clearance, turn the engine over until No. 1 tappet is fully raised. In like manner, check No. 3 when No. 4 is up, No. 4 when No. 3 is up, No. 5 when No. 6 is up, and so on. In other words, to check the clearances for each cylinder, one tappet must be raised while the other one belonging to the same cylinder is being checked.

When examining tappet clearances note should be made of

any cylinder where no tappet clearance is found at one or both of the tappets, and after the clearance has been correctly adjusted, the compression of this cylinder should be tested by slowly

Fig. 31. Showing Cylinder and Tappet Numbers
The firing order is also indicated.

turning over the starting handle. If no substantial resistance to motion is felt, it is probable—in fact almost certain—that compression leakage is occurring past the valves, and an early opportunity should be taken of inspecting the valves and their seatings, especially in the case of the exhaust valves which have probably become pitted or scaled and will require grinding-in. Always bear in mind that too small or complete absence of tappet clearances are likely to cause actual damage to the valves, whereas excessive clearances are unlikely to do more than create undue noise and inefficiency. Having overhauled the tappets, make sure before replacing the valve chest cover plate that the joint in its washer is at the top, otherwise some oil leakage from the valve chest may occur.

When to Decarbonize. The remarks given under this heading on page 37 concerning the air-cooled engine are applicable to the water-cooled engine also. *About once every* 5,000 *miles* the monobloc cylinder head should be removed, and all carbon deposits scraped from the combustion chambers and ports and from the tops of the pistons. Decarbonizing, however, which is a process capable of being performed by anyone single-handed, need not be attended to until some of the recognized symptoms caused by carbon deposits such as pinking, loss of power, and roughness of running begin to appear.

Warm Up the Cylinder Head First. Before starting on the job of decarbonizing, it is a good plan to start the engine and let it tick over for several minutes. This will not only circulate and warm up the oil with the result that the pistons leave the cylinder block somewhat more readily, but it will also warm up the cylinder head which will retain the heat throughout the process of decarbonizing and consequently be more pleasant to handle. Further, it will be found more easy to remove the carbon when warm.

Preliminary Decarbonizing Operations. Removal of the bonnet is not an essential preliminary to decarbonizing, but owing to the greater accessibility thereby afforded, its removal is recommended. To remove the bonnet, remove the nut from the forward end of the horizontal tie rod E (Fig. 30), and swing the radiator forward approximately half an inch until the central bonnet hinge pin emerges from its socket I on the upper edge of the scuttle. The bonnet can then be lifted off and placed carefully on one side, standing it on end.

Having removed the bonnet, drain the whole of the cooling water from the engine and radiator by removing the plug at the rear of the latter just above the front index number plate C (Fig. 30). Then slacken off the water hose clip D at the cylinder head end and withdraw the water hose from the cylinder head stub.

Next, disconnect the petrol pipe union, being careful not to lose the small gauze filter inside when withdrawing it. The carburettor can now be removed by unscrewing the two induction flange nuts and also the nut on the inner side of the throttle control arm at F (Fig. 30).

The induction and exhaust manifolds can now be simultaneously taken off if the securing nuts are first removed. One of the nuts is shown at G (Fig. 30).

After detaching the H.T. plug cables at the sparking plug

terminals and drawing them aside, remove the plugs, and the cylinder head is then ready to be tackled.

Removing Cylinder Head. To resist the high explosion pressures, the cylinder head nuts are necessarily screwed up very tight, and it is very important to avoid straining or distortion of the monobloc head that the seventeen nuts holding it down on the cylinder are unscrewed strictly according to the order given in Fig. 32. Unscrew each nut in rotation half a turn at first, then

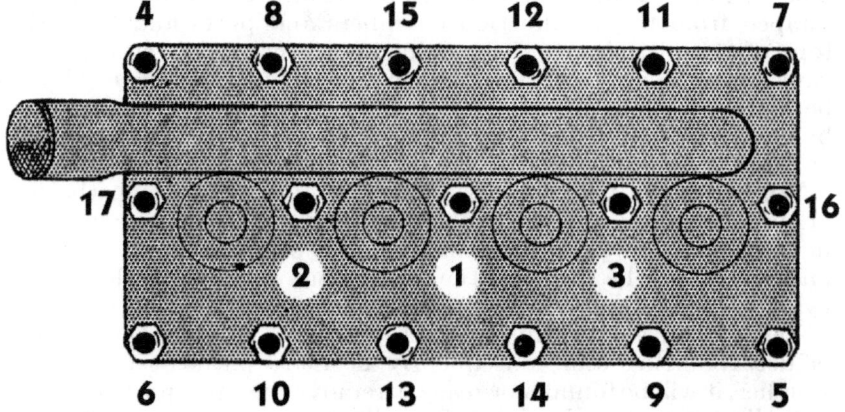

Fig. 32. The Correct Order for Tightening or Loosening the Cylinder Head Nuts

a complete turn, and finally, starting at No. 1 and finishing at No. 17, unscrew each nut completely. To break the cylinder head joint tap all round the edge lightly with a lead or wood mallet, and then tap in an upward direction the three projections along the lower edge of the head. Grasp the water hose stub and then apply a gentle rocking movement which should free the head completely and allow it to be lifted clear of the studs without difficulty. Place it carefully on the ground or any safe position, as the slightest fall is liable to crack the brittle material of which it is composed. Also cover the cylinder block openings with a piece of clean rag.

Valve Removal. This is not necessary to decarbonize, since on the water-cooled side-valve engine the valves are below the level of the detachable head, but valve removal is advised whenever it becomes necessary to remove the head so that the valves may be examined and, if necessary, ground-in. On no account should the valves be interchanged, and to avoid mixing them up the valves are numbered 1 to 8, counting from the radiator (see Fig. 31). As an additional safeguard, it is a good plan to remove them, grind them in, and replace them one at a time.

MAINTENANCE AND OVERHAUL

To remove the valves, first take off the valve chest cover plate, as described on page 48, and then remove each valve in the following simple manner. Apply the forked end of the special lever supplied in the tool kit to the valve spring cap as illustrated in Fig. 33. so that it clears the cotter A, and rest the bracket on the lever on the side of the valve chest. The valve spring can now be compressed by downward pressure at B, and the "U" shaped cotter may readily be pulled out with a small pair of pliers.

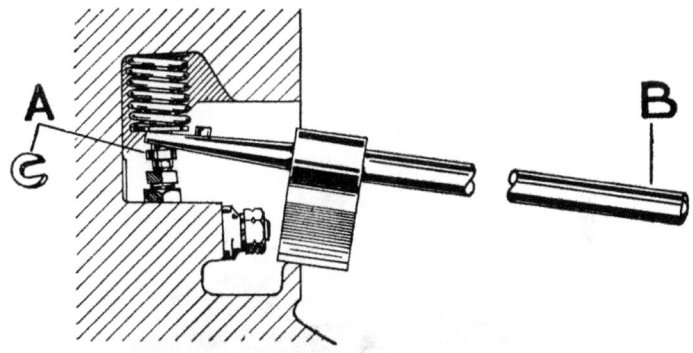

Fig. 33. How to Use the B.S.A. Valve Spring Compressor.

Should the act of compressing the valve spring lift the valve, it should be tapped down gently on to its seating. As soon as the cotter is removed, the spring with its collars can be drawn off and the valve lifted upwards out of its guide.

Another method of compressing the valve spring is to use a proprietary make of valve spring compressor. A good example is shown in Fig. 33A. The hooked end is placed so that it rests on the centre of the valve head and the other end is slipped between the valve spring collar and cotter. By pressing the lever down in the direction indicated by the arrow the spring is compressed and may be kept thus by engaging the pointed end of the smaller lever X with one of the notches in the upright arm.

Decarbonizing. Decarbonizing the cylinder head is quite an easy job. It is only necessary to lay the cylinder head block down in an inverted position and chip and scrape off all carbon deposits from the four combustion chambers and from the edges and lower threads of the sparking plug holes. *On no account use emery cloth or any abrasive on the machined joint face* which is in contact with the cylinder head gasket. Finally, clean the whole of the interior of the head and the base with a rag dipped in petrol or paraffin.

To decarbonize the pistons the engine should be rotated slowly with the starting handle until Nos. 1 and 4 pistons are on T.D.C.

54   THE BOOK OF THE B.S.A. THREE WHEELER

Then stuff some clean rag into Nos. 2 and 3 cylinders and with an old screwdriver or blunt chisel carefully scrape off all carbon deposits from the crowns of Nos. 1 and 4 pistons (see Fig. 34). When doing this avoid scratching the piston surfaces with the edge of the screwdriver and afterwards do not polish with emery cloth. If any final polishing is desired, this should be done most carefully with metal polish as suggested on page 41 for the air-cooled engines. Any polish that might get between the piston

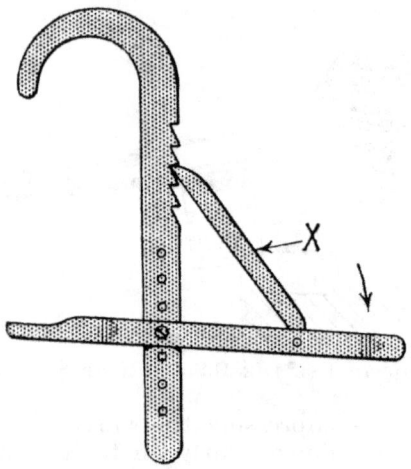

FIG. 33A. GOOD PROPRIETARY VALVE SPRING COMPRESSOR—
THE TERRY

and cylinder would tend to lap out the cylinder bore with disastrous effect. Also, remove any carbon which may have accumulated on top of the cylinder block (integral with the crankcase) around the valves. Here, again, beware using any emery cloth. Having removed all carbon deposits, wipe the surfaces with an oily or paraffin rag. After decarbonizing Nos. 1 and 4 pistons, remove the rags from Nos. 2 and 3 cylinders and rotate the engine until the two centre pistons are on T.D.C. Then insert rags into Nos. 1 and 4 and decarbonize Nos. 2 and 3 pistons as described above.

Grinding-in the Valves. If any valves are *badly* pitted no attempt should be made to grind them in for reasons stated on page 43, and they should be sent to the B.S.A. works at Birmingham to be refaced. On their return it will be found necessary to grind them in only slightly in order to make them seat perfectly.

To grind-in *slightly* pitted overhead valves, the procedure is much the same as for side-valves (described on page 43), but in this case, instead of a special tool being used to pull the valves against their seats, the valves are simultaneously pressed down

MAINTENANCE AND OVERHAUL 55

on their seats and rotated with wrist action by means of a screwdriver, or screwdriver-shaped bit held in a brace, inserted in each valve head slot.

Using fine grinding paste, rotate each valve backwards and forwards by a turn of the wrist. Every few strokes lift the valve slightly off its seat and move it to a different position to prevent the formation of "rings." It will facilitate lifting the valve if a small compression spring be slipped under the valve head as

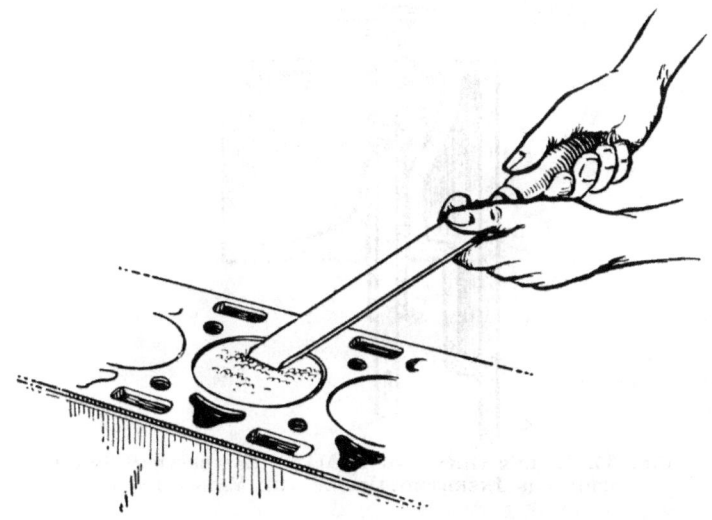

FIG. 34. REMOVING CARBON DEPOSITS FROM PISTONS

shown diagrammatically in Fig. 35. It will then only be necessary to remove the pressure on the screwdriver in order to lift the valve. Valve grinding should be continued until an inspection of each valve face shows a perfectly smooth and bright surface all round. A method of testing valves after grinding-in has already been described on page 44.

After grinding-in the valves *take the greatest care to remove all traces of the grinding paste* from both the valves and their seats in the cylinder block, and before refitting the valves and replacing their springs, collars, and cotters, smear the valve stems with a little clean oil. Replace any valve springs which have lost their strength (see page 45). Finally check and, if necessary, adjust the tappet clearances as described on page 48.

Reassembly. Repeat the process described for dismantling in the reverse order, but before replacing the cylinder head examine the gasket washer for any defects. Do not replace the old gasket over the studs if there are any doubts as to its soundness, but fit a new one. Black or badly stained patches, particularly between the cylinder bores, indicate that there is blow or gas leakage occurring.

Having carefully placed the cylinder head over the studs, refit all the seventeen nuts and screw them down until they are just in contact with the head. Then tighten them up half a turn at a time in the order indicated in Fig. 32. Do the nuts up thoroughly

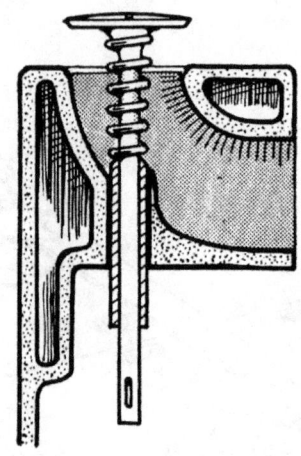

Fig. 35. Valve Grinding is Made Easier if a Small Spring is Inserted Under the Valve Head

tight but do not give any powerful hammer blows for final tightening. Reasonably gentle taps are all that is necessary. Refit the plugs, H.T. leads, manifolds, carburettor, petrol pipe, hose, and replace the bonnet. After the engine has been restarted and warmed up, expansion may cause the cylinder head nuts to slacken a trifle and an additional fraction of a turn should be given them. It is, in fact, wise after dismantling to run up the engine until quite warm, and then check over the tightness of the various nuts which have been previously removed or loosened. Also, do not forget to check the tappet adjustment after about 50 miles' running, following grinding-in of the valves. This has already been referred to on page 48.

Attention to Pistons and Rings. A mileage of at least 20,000 should be completed before it becomes necessary to remove the pistons for examination. Provided that the engine gives a satisfactory performance, it may be presumed that the pistons and rings do not require attention. However, any loss of compression which cannot be traced to the valves or cylinder head joint, will indicate that the time has arrived when piston and possibly

MAINTENANCE AND OVERHAUL

cylinder overhaul is necessary. This evil day can be greatly postponed by careful driving and regular attention to lubrication, decarbonizing, and valve grinding.

Some Skill is Required to Remove Pistons. Piston removal is an operation not to be lightly undertaken by those lacking in mechanical sense or gifted with "clumsy hands." The author (and also Messrs. B.S.A., Ltd.) recommends that when attention to the pistons is necessary, the work be entrusted to the nearest B.S.A. dealer.

For the benefit of mechanically-minded persons who wish to remove the pistons themselves, the following information is given:
1. Remove the plugs.
2. Drain the sump and remove by undoing 16 nuts and tapping off.
3. Revolve engine until a piston is on B.D.C.
4. Remove split cotter pins from big-end bolts.
5. Unscrew big-end bolts and pull cap off.
6. Revolve engine another three-quarters of a turn.
7. Draw out from the underneath the connecting-rod and piston.
8. Undo small-end pinch bolt.
9. Tap out non-floating gudgeon-pin.

Deal as above with each of the four pistons. It should be observed that as soon as the big-end cap is pulled off and the engine is rotated another three-quarters of a turn the connecting-rod automatically clears the crankshaft and enables the connecting-rod and piston to be drawn clear of the cylinder bore. The most satisfactory method of removing the gudgeon-pins is to insert a small plug at both ends of each pin and then to grip the pin between the jaws of a vice as shown in Fig. 36. This will greatly facilitate the removal and replacement of the pinch bolt.

The crankshaft assembly is balanced with great precision, and this balance must never be interfered with. All four connecting rods are carefully matched in weight and should it be necessary to fit a new rod, one should be obtained which bears the same mark on the bolt boss as the original one (i.e. " + ," "0," or " – ").

Resetting Ignition Timing. This will be necessary if for any reason the distributor has been removed and should be done in the following manner—

Take out the sparking plug from No. 1 cylinder and also remove the filling plug from over the clutch pit (Fig. 49). Then slowly revolve the engine with the starting handle and, looking through the sparking plug hole, note exactly when the exhaust valve (which is the right-hand valve, looking from the distributor side of the engine) closes. It will be observed that a mark on the fly-wheel appears under the clutch filler plug hole as soon as the exhaust valve returns to its seat. Now rotate the engine one more revolution until the mark appears again, when it will be found that the piston of No. 1 cylinder is on T.D.C. on the compression stroke. Carefully set the distributor arm in the position shown in Fig. 37, and then gently replace the distributor so that the flat side *A* is parallel with the engine and away from it. The distributor arm will be seen to turn slightly as the distributor gear meshes with the driving gear. Before tightening

Fig. 36. Gudgeon-pin Held in Vice for Pinch Bolt Removal

the locking screw *B*, ascertain that the points of the contact-breaker are just commencing to break. The gap at the contacts should not exceed ·004 in., and it should be checked with the inlet tappet gauge provided in the tool kit. To correct the gap if necessary, slowly move the body of the distributor clockwise or anti-clockwise until the ·004 in. gauge just enters the gap without binding. It may be found that this adjustment of the contacts cannot be found with only slight movement of the distributor body, and in this case it will be necessary to withdraw the distributor and reset on another gear tooth. The foregoing sounds a trifle complicated, but in practice it is not. This should be verified after the first 1000 miles' running, and subsequently, if indifferent running is experienced, because the contact-breaker beds down slightly. Put briefly, the above instructions amount to this—

1. Set the contact-breaker points to the ignition spanner gauge with contacts wide open.

2. Adjust the contacts to open ·004 in. at T.D.C.

Why accurate Ignition Timing is Essential. Really satisfactory

MAINTENANCE AND OVERHAUL

running on any car cannot be expected unless the ignition timing is accurately set. This applies with special force to the B.S.A. cars which have automatically-controlled ignition and no manual adjustment for correcting any error in timing. The driver relies entirely upon the functioning of the automatic control, and the

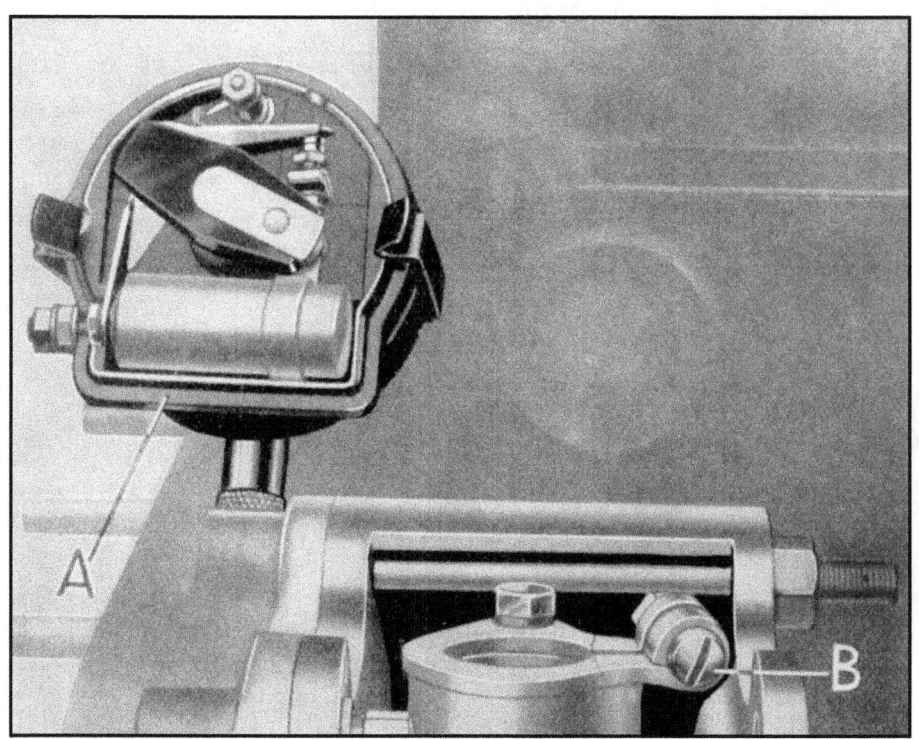

FIG. 37. SHOWING POSITION OF DISTRIBUTOR ARM FOR CORRECT IGNITION TIMING

power output may be seriously affected if the setting is not made accurately in the first place.

The ignition spanner gauge should just pass between the contact-breaker points when wide open. Retarded ignition will be caused if the gap between them becomes reduced due to wear on the fibre heel of the contact-breaker arm, and the locknut on the fixed contact should be loosened and the contact screwed home until the gap is correct. It is incidentally quite as important that the gap should not be excessive as it is that it should not be too small, but this contingency is not very likely to happen. Two degrees difference in ignition timing is caused by one-thousandth of an inch error in the gap at the contacts. As in the case of the air-cooled models, the use of special fuels and special road conditions sometimes justify a greater ignition advance than the standard setting already described, but the average owner should not depart from this setting.

To Adjust Dynamo Chain. As may be seen in Fig. 38, a single

Fig. 38. Showing Arrangement of Camshaft and Dynamo Drive (Four-cylinder)

chain is used to drive both the camshaft and the dynamo. This chain being in the timing case is always well lubricated and kept free of dirt. Wear and stretch therefore take place very slowly indeed.

Should any slackness develop after a big mileage, the chain may be adjusted by slackening the three nuts on the dynamo and distributor bracket and moving the unit slightly outwards to tighten, or inwards to slacken. After making an adjustment, carefully retighten the nuts.

MAINTENANCE AND OVERHAUL   61

Correct Valve Setting. If the engine is taken down for a thorough overhaul, or if the dynamo chain is completely removed from the three sprockets, it is necessary to see that the valve

FIG. 39. CAMSHAFT AND OIL PUMP DRIVE (TWIN-CYLINDER)

timing is correctly reset. This is very simple, as the designer of the engine has employed a system of marking whereby it is virtually impossible to make an error if reasonable care is taken. Fig. 38 is self-explanatory and requires practically no comment. As may be seen, the valve timing is correct when the chain is replaced with the camshaft sprocket arrow facing the **arrow** marked on the adjacent rectangular boss, and the piston in No. 1 cylinder is in the top dead centre position on the compression stroke.

Fig. 39 shows the timing gear of the air-cooled model. The valve timing is correct when the teeth of the gear wheels **marked** with a line are in mesh and the piston in No. 1 cylinder is in top dead centre position on the exhaust stroke.

THE CARBURETTOR

Solex carburettors are used on both the air-cooled and water-cooled Three Wheelers. In general design and principle they are

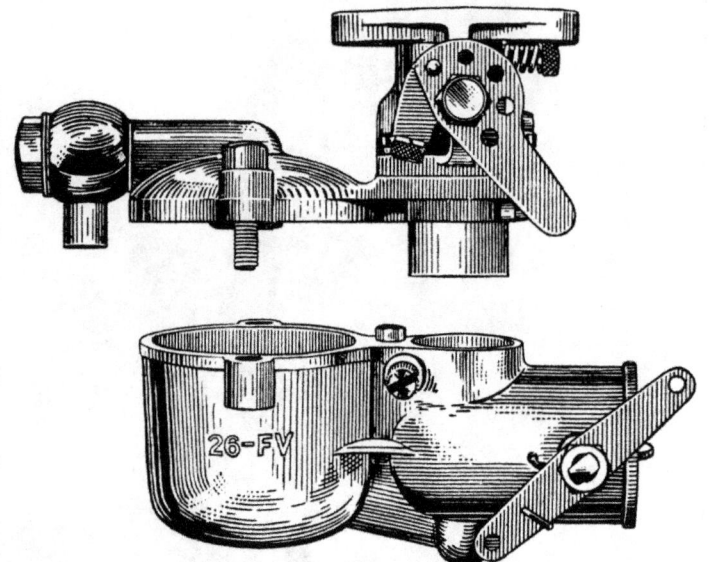

Fig. 40. Vertical Type Solex Carburettor with Float Chamber Detached (F.V.)
The upper half can be detached from the lower half by the removal of two bolts.

similar, and tuning and dismantling instructions apply to both types of carburettor fitted by the B.S.A. manufacturers. The difference between the two types are that in the case of the carburettor fitted to the air-cooled engines the arrangement of the engine manifolds and induction system requires a vertical type carburettor, whereas the four-cylinder water-cooled engine requires a horizontal type carburettor. Also, the horizontal type is provided with a kind of auxiliary carburettor known as a "Starter" instead of the strangler provided in the case of the vertical type carburettor. The point to be noted is that, except for starting purposes, the starter device plays no part, and the two types of carburettor may be regarded as the same. Both the strangler and the starter device are designed to ensure a rich mixture for starting *from cold*. The latter is entirely automatic in action as it depends on engine suction and has a separate jet and mixing chamber drawing its fuel supply from the main float chamber.

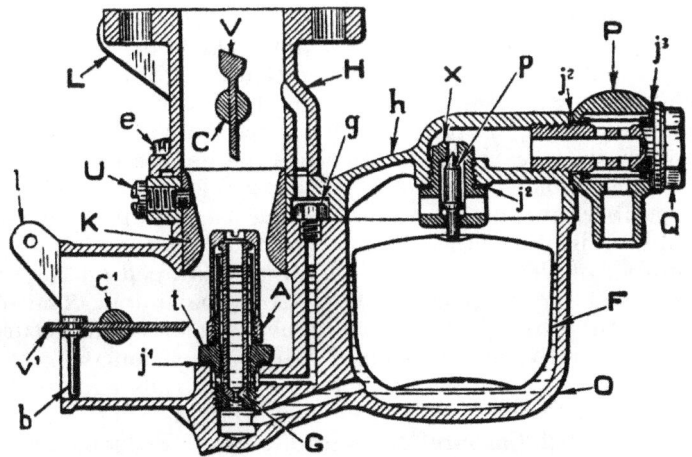

FIG. 41. SECTIONAL VIEW OF CARBURETTOR SHOWN IN FIG. 40

KEY TO FIG. 41

A = Main jet cap
b = Strangler shutter stop
C = Throttle spindle
C^1 = Strangler shutter spindle
e = Body assembling screw
F = Float
G = Main jet
g = Auxiliary jet
H = Throttle chamber
h = Carburettor body
J^1 = Main jet carrier washer
J^2 = Needle valve and small filter union washer
J^3 = Large filter union washer
K = Choke tube
L = Throttle lever
l = Strangler lever
O = Float chamber
P = Swivelling filter union
Q = Filter union nut
t = Main jet carrier
U = Choke tube fixing screw
V = Butterfly
V^1 = Strangler shutter
X = Needle valve seating

How to Remove the Float Chamber. To remove the float chamber and the jets also for cleaning or adjustment is a simple matter with the Solex carburettor owing to its peculiarly neat and simple design. As may be seen in Figs. 40, 41, it is only necessary to remove two screws to enable the float chamber, complete with float and both the jets, to be detached. When refitting the lower half of the carburettor, make sure that the main and auxiliary jets register correctly in their places and afterwards tighten the securing bolts e moderately tight.

As regards the upper half of the carburettor, this is not made in one piece, but it is neither advisable nor necessary to break the joints. All tuning and adjustments can be carried out with the upper half of the instrument left permanently attached by its flange to the induction manifold. The upper half or main body of the carburettor comprises two parts. One part houses the throttle V (Fig. 41), and the other constitutes the main body of the carburettor and top of the float chamber H containing the needle p, the petrol union filter P, and the choke tube K. This applies to both the vertical and horizontal carburettors.

Carburettor Replacements. In the event of any carburettor replacements being required, certain particulars should be supplied when sending the order to the manufacturers. Some parts such as the choke tube, main jet, main jet cap, auxiliary jet, float chamber, and needle valve seating are stamped with one or more numerals and these must be quoted, together with the size and number of the carburettor which are stamped on the outside of the float chamber below the petrol pipe union. The size of the choke tube and jets and also the date of manufacture and horse-power of the engine should also be mentioned.

In the case of unnumbered parts it is quite sufficient to indicate the works number and size of the carburettor.

Do Not Adjust Carburettor Without Good Reason. Many car owners, particularly those of a tinkering nature, are tempted to meddle with the carburettor with the object of improving performance. Disappointment usually follows for an obvious reason, namely, that the carburettor is adjusted with very great care by the manufacturers following a series of road and bench tests. Very seldom can better results be obtained by altering this setting which is intended for a good all-round performance in a temperate climate at an altitude of less than 3,000 ft. and for ordinary fuel obtainable from petrol pumps. It is wise, therefore, not to alter the standard setting without good reason, i.e. unless you contemplate a trip in mountainous country or in tropical regions.

There are Five Means of Adjustment. First, there is the size of the choke tube K (Fig. 42), which controls the volume of air, then there is the size of the main jet G for obtaining normal running mixture, and, lastly, the auxiliary jet g for the idling mixture and the slow-running adjustment screw Z, together with the auxiliary mixture regulating screw W (Fig. 43).

To remove the choke tube, remove the bell in the case of the horizontal (F.H.) carburettor, and loosen the choke tube fixing screw situated at the upper part of the body on the F.H. carburettor

KEY TO FIG. 42

A = Main jet cap
a = Throttle stop screw
D = Spindle end nut
F = Float
G = Main jet
g = Auxiliary jet
H = Throttle chamber
h = Body of carburettor
h^1 = Starter body
I^1 = Starter lever
J^1 = Main jet carrier washer
J^2 and J^3 = Filter union washers
J^4 = Washers for base plug
K = Choke tube
L = Throttle lever
N = Starter pipe
O = Float chamber
P = Swivelling filter union
Q = Filter union nut
R = Base plug
S = Abutment plate
T = Tickler
t = Main jet carrier
U = Choke tube fixing screw
V = Butterfly
X = Needle valve
Z = Slow-running screw

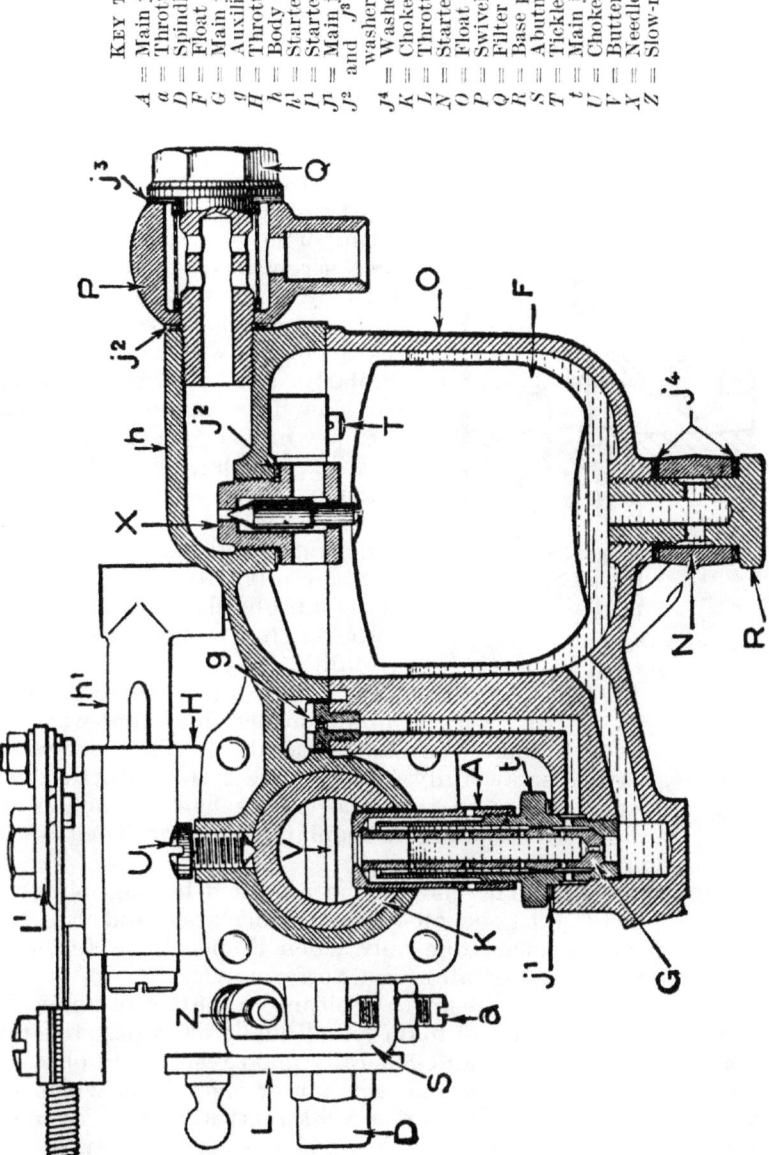

FIG. 42. SECTIONAL VIEW OF HORIZONTAL TYPE, SELF-STARTING SOLEX CARBURETTOR

and at the side in the case of the vertical (F.V.) carburettor, when the choke tube itself may readily be withdrawn. When replacing the choke tube, see that the choke tube numbers indicative of size and type are stamped at the atmospheric side in the case of the F.H. and at the bottom in the case of the F.V. carburettor. To remove the main jet, it is only necessary to remove the jet cap. The auxiliary jet can be removed by unscrewing it.

Adjusting for Slow Running. The auxiliary jet g (Fig. 43) is concerned with tick-over and its size has been selected very carefully. The rate of idling is determined by the closing of the throttle, and this is limited by the setting of the slow-running adjustment screw Z (Fig. 42) mounted on the abutment plate. By rotating the screw clockwise, the engine tick-over revs will be accelerated. Similarly, anti-clockwise rotation will slow the engine down. The auxiliary mixture regulating screw W (Fig. 43) is incorporated in addition to the slow-running adjustment screw with the object of regulating within certain limits the auxiliary mixture strength which, unless absolutely correct, results in the engine tending to "hunt" or stall.

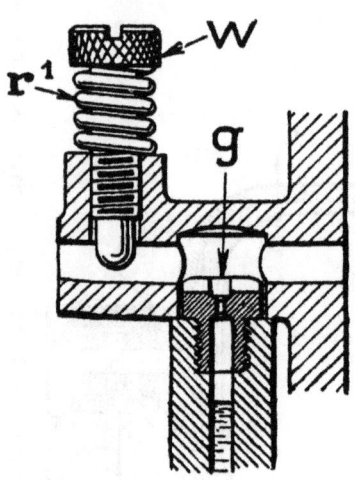

FIG. 43. SECTION OF AUXILIARY MIXTURE REGULATING SCREW ON HORIZONTAL CARBURETTOR

To obtain the correct slow-running adjustment, first warm up the engine to the normal working temperature. Then screw the mixture regulating screw fully home and set the throttle slow-running adjusting screw so that the engine has a tendency to "hunt." Now rotate the mixture regulating screw anti-clockwise until the engine ticks over regularly.

Tuning for Power. The choke tube provided in the Solex carburettor is chosen for good all-round performance and it is best to change it for another one only when a specific performance is desired, irrespective of all-round performance.

Tuning for power then resolves itself into a matter of determining the most suitable size of main jet. Usually it is best to select as small a jet as possible, and generally good results are obtained by choosing a jet which is one size larger than that which obviously gives a poor mixture, i.e. a weak mixture which is readily discernible by the tendency for blowback through the carburettor on opening the throttle. Symptoms of an over rich mixture are rapid sooting up of the plugs, high fuel consumption, and a tendency for exhaust banging. When carburation is correct, the colour of the porcelains should be approximately chestnut. It should be noted, however, that when carburation is right for the summer months it is often a little poor during the cold winter months on account of less complete vaporization. In this case it is generally wise to fit a main jet one, or perhaps two, sizes larger. When tuning for speed, fuel consumption can, of course, be disregarded.

Main Jet Size. Two numbers are provided on the side of the main jet tube. The first (74, for example) indicates the diameter of the fuel metering orifice (i.e. the lowest hole) in hundredths of millimetres, and the second (40, for example) indicates the disposition and number of the lateral correction holes. On no account reamer out any of the jet holes, because correction holes of corresponding calibrations are required and experimental work of this kind is within the sphere of carburation specialists, not amateurs.

DIAGNOSING CARBURETTOR FAULTS

The Solex carburettor seldom gives much trouble and, provided the adjustment is not tampered with unnecessarily and the fuel supply system is occasionally cleaned and the various joints kept tight, there is no reason why any trouble should develop. The majority of engine failures are due to ignition troubles and these are dealt with in Chapter VII. If the engine will not start or runs badly don't first put the blame on the Solex carburettor You will almost certainly be wrong.

Causes of Flooding. Flooding of the carburettor which persists is not only most aggravating because of the bad running it gives rise to, but is also most wasteful and possibly dangerous. There are four possible causes of slight or extensive flooding, namely— (1) Loose joints in the supply system; (2) grit on the needle seating; (3) a punctured float; (4) fuel level too high. Dealing with them in this order—

1. Loose Joints. The self-starting Solex carburettor has only six joints and the first thing that should be done when a carburettor floods is to see that these joints are absolutely tight. Since they are exterior this is quite simple. The six joints comprise the joint of the main jet carrier, the joint of the needle valve, the joints of the petrol union, the joints in the petrol pipe exterior to the carburettor, and, lastly, the joints in the base plug connecting the starter to the float chamber.

2. Grit on the Needle Seating. This is most unlikely to occur, for all B.S.A. cars have an adequate filter which does not allow grit to enter the carburettor, except in minute particles. Sometimes, however, some stray particles of packing material, or oxide, or solder from the petrol pipe do find their way in and interfere with the needle valve by preventing the needle seating perfectly. Under such circumstances the remedy is to remove the needle valve and clean it by carefully blowing it out and noting by suction test that it is hermetic. Afterwards replace it and be sure that the washer is perfect and the tightening adequate.

3. Punctured Float. Leakage of petrol past the jets will obviously occur immediately any petrol gets into the carburettor float thereby increasing its weight. The remedy is to fit a new float or else solder the point of leakage on the old one. To do this is rather a skilled job and only the smallest amount of solder must be used to patch up the float. To prevent the tendency for the float to swim on an uneven keel, it would probably be necessary to put a blob of solder also on the opposite side. To locate the leakage, immerse the float in boiling water and note the place from where air bubbles arise.

4. Fuel Level Too High. This trouble also is unlikely because the simplicity of the level controlling arrangements in the Solex is such that the level is sure to be correct unless the adjustment has been disturbed by someone to enable heavy commercial petrol to be used, in which case the obvious remedy is to revert to a lighter fuel or fit a washer under the needle valve. The float weights determined for ·730 petrol are 26 grammes for 26 and 30 mm. carburettors, and 65 grammes for 35 and 40 mm. carburettors.

To check the fuel level it is only necessary to remove the float chamber, main jet cap and jet G, leaving the jet carrier in position, after which the float chamber is replaced facing the opposite direction, so that the jet carrier is exposed outside the choke tube, when the level of the fuel in the jet can be observed.

Difficulty in Starting. Where ignition trouble is not suspected, and, indeed, whenever the engine refuses work, it is advisable to assure yourself from the beginning that the petrol tap is turned on and that there is fuel left in the tank. It is surprising how many people work themselves into a frenzy and then find that the tap was off. If there is a stoppage in the supply system with the tap on, examine the filter and, if necessary, clean it (see page 73). Also, if the obstruction persists, remove the fuel pipe and blow it clear. Sometimes an air lock is responsible for fuel not reaching the carburettor in sufficient quantities. This can be cured by removal of the pipe and priming, or by the temporary application of air pressure to the filler cap. Vapour locks can also be caused by a fuel pipe too near the exhaust manifold.

Bad Slow Running. If the engine will not tick-over nicely, the first thing to do is to ascertain that the adjustment is correct. Should good slow running still be unobtainable, air leaks at some point in the induction system should be suspected. The most likely place is at the inlet valve guides. Bad leakages here quickly ruin slow running. Try a slightly larger auxiliary jet, but not too large, otherwise the engine will "hunt" while idling. When deciding between two jets giving approximately the same results, always give preference to the larger one. But, before interfering with the jet, make quite sure that the jet is clear of any obstruction.

If uniform slow running cannot be obtained in spite of experimenting with various auxiliary jets, excessive induction leakage is almost certainly occurring, assuming that the valve timing and ignition are in order.

THE CHASSIS

Exactly the same type of chassis is used for both the air-cooled O.H.V. twin-cylinder B.S.A. models as for the S.V. four-cylinder models with the exception, of course, that in the former case a dummy radiator is provided, and in the case of the latter a honeycomb block type radiator is fitted. The following notes on running adjustments and dismantling therefore apply to all models with the above exception.

Keep the Brakes Adjusted Correctly. If maximum braking effect and freedom from skidding are to be obtained it is absolutely essential that the brakes be kept correctly adjusted. A spring box is incorporated in the rear brake rod in order to balance the brake pressures evenly and so ensure efficiency and stability on dangerous road surfaces, but this might just as well be a mousetrap unless the correct brake adjustment is maintained! The footbrake pedal operates the front and rear brakes by means of a pick-up lever, and as may be seen in Fig. 44, there are two wing nuts for adjustment. The upper one controls the rear brake adjustment and the lower one the front brake adjustment. The important thing is to co-ordinate the front and rear brake action by suitable adjustment of the wing nuts. The correct adjustment is obtained when a test shows that (a) the rear wheel is free when the front wheels are just tight, and (b) the front wheels are locked solid when it is just possible to move the rear wheel. In other words, the front brake must come into action before the rear one. The best way to test the adjustment is to depress the brake pedal while an assistant tries the front wheels and then the rear wheel.

How to Adjust the Clutch. The clutch may need adjusting after a considerable mileage has been covered. To do this, slacken off the nut at the front end of the clutch actuating rod,

70 THE BOOK OF THE B.S.A. THREE WHEELER

and slide the lever a little along the slot provided at this point. The adjustment should be such that when the clutch is fully disengaged there is ½-in. clearance between the pedal and floorboard of the air-cooled models, and the same clearance between the pedal and timing cover of the water-cooled models.

Shock Absorber Adjustment. To adjust the rear shock absorber which is fitted to the rear wheel arm at the near side of the

FIG. 44. THE BRAKE PICK-UP LEVER AND THE WING NUT ADJUSTMENT

trunnion bracket, release the locknut with the box spanner supplied in the tool kit, and then with an adjustable spanner turn the larger hexagon nut clockwise or anti-clockwise as required.

To adjust the front wheel shock absorbers, release the locknuts and screw in or out the inner nuts as required. Carefully tighten the locknuts after making an adjustment.

Shock absorbers are provided for the purpose of retarding spring deflection and preventing violent rebound, and naturally the best adjustment depends largely upon driving methods and road conditions. Fast driving over rough surfaces requires a high pressure, while slow driving over smooth surfaces requires

MAINTENANCE AND OVERHAUL

a low pressure. The shock absorbers are adjusted at the B.S.A. works for normal pressure, and a slight adjustment should suffice to cover a wide range of road conditions. It is well worth while spending a little time making an adjustment to the shock absorber pressure to meet your personal requirements. Should the normal shock absorber adjustment be lost, screw the adjuster right out until the star washer is just free and then screw the adjuster in again two turns.

It should be noted that the pressure of the rear wheel shock absorber should not be excessively reduced, and the adjustment should be made carefully and maintained, otherwise the road holding and steering qualities of the car may be seriously impaired.

Wheel Removal. Detachable wire wheels are fitted to all B.S.A. models, and their removal and refitting is quite simple if the correct procedure is followed.

To remove a front wheel, place under the two front wheel springs as near to the wheel as possible the special bridge piece supplied in the tool kit and insert in it the top of the jack. Now screw the jack up and unscrew the four nuts with the special brace provided, when it will be possible to remove the wheel. It should be noted that the nuts on the near-side front wheel and the rear wheel have left-hand threads and are marked "L" to identify them. Their removal therefore necessitates clockwise turning. Those on the offside front wheel have right-hand threads, and to remove them counter-clockwise rotation is required. To simplify front wheel removal it is best to jack up the axle so that, although the weight of the car is removed, the tyre treads are still in contact with the ground. This will prevent wheel rotation, but, of course, prior to wheel replacement it may be necessary to raise the axle slightly more so as to counteract the tyre expansion after full inflation.

A quickly detachable rear mudguard is fitted on certain models, and to remove this it is only necessary to raise the locker lid and detach the quick-release wing nuts which retain the guard, which can then be lifted out.

Rear wheel removal entails inserting the top of the jack in the socket formed in the jack pad of the rear wheel and placing the block of wood supplied in the tool kit between the ground and the bottom of the jack to prevent the latter slipping out of place.

With regard to the actual unscrewing of the wheel nuts, it may be mentioned that in the case of the models provided with detachable rear mudguards, it is best to apply the brace from the inside of the locker and to lift the wheel out through the locker (see Fig. 45.) On certain models the wheel brace should be applied to the nuts from the under side of the body.

72   THE BOOK OF THE B.S.A. THREE WHEELER

To refit a wheel it is only necessary to lift it into place and carefully retighten the four securing nuts with the brace and afterwards spin the wheel to ensure that it runs true. Do not forget to check over the tightness of the nuts again after a short mileage.

Ball Joints in Steering Gear. Should the steering cross rod and track rod ball joints be disturbed, it is of vital importance

FIG. 45. SHOWING HOW REAR WHEEL IS REMOVED
(Mudguard partly removed.)

on reassembly that the screwed end plugs should be screwed up solid and then slackened back just enough to allow the split pins to be inserted. *Under no circumstances should this slackening exceed half a turn.*

Be Careful With Radiator. Although the honeycomb radiator on the four-cylinder models appears substantial enough, actually it is very fragile and should be treated with due respect. The front honeycomb acts as a guard for the cooling channels immediately behind, but there is no protection on the inside of this. Therefore, avoid letting any tools strike the radiator honeycomb, since a heavy blow may start a leakage.

MAINTENANCE AND OVERHAUL

Protection Against Freezing. In very cold weather (i.e. when the mercury remains at or below freezing point for some days) the radiator should be either (*a*) drained, or (*b*) filled with an anti-freezing mixture to prevent the formation of ice in the water jackets and radiator when the car is left standing for some time, because during expansion of the water in the act of becoming ice serious damage may be caused. The use of an anti-freezing mixture is, perhaps, the simplest protection against freezing.

At the commencement of the winter, some of one of the numerous brands of special anti-freezing preparations should be added to the cooling water. Ordinary commercial glycerine is quite suitable, and if this is used it should be added in the proportions of 3 *pints of glycerine to* 2 *gal. of water.* Incidentally, the B.S.A. tankage is approximately 2 gal., and therefore it is only necessary to drain off 3 pints of water *via* the plug at the base of the honeycomb block within the bonnet (an amount of water equivalent to the glycerine), and pour in 3 pints of glycerine.

Always Maintain Radiator Water Level. Some drivers during bitterly cold weather fit a radiator muff to maintain the radiator and engine temperature while running. This is sound practice, but the habit of driving with a depleted water supply must not be adopted in the case of a thermo-siphon system such as is used on B.S.A. cars. The water in the radiator should always be maintained *within an inch of the filling orifice*, and as soon as the level falls, the supply should be replenished. Hard water should be boiled before insertion, otherwise chemical impurities may accumulate and later cause obstructions in the honeycomb.

Causes of Boiling. The radiator water should not boil under normal circumstances, for the water supply is quite adequate for satisfactory cooling. If it does boil (and the level is correct), the boiling may be caused by exceptionally severe road conditions, undue running on the lower gears, faulty ignition, or incorrect carburation (see pages 62 to 69), or else to some mechanical defect which should be immediately looked to.

Water Hose Connections on a New Car. After a few miles running on a new car the water hose connections should be examined for signs of slight leakage which may occur. To rectify matters, tighten up the clips slightly.

Cleaning Petrol Filter. The petrol filter situated at the top of the carburettor float chamber at the petrol pipe union is responsible for trapping impurities which might choke up the carburettor jets, and *at least once or twice during the year* the filter gauze should be cleaned of all impurities which may have collected. To remove the gauze, unscrew the hexagon-headed plug in front of the pipe union, when it will be found that the gauze comes away with it. On reassembling the filter do not forget to replace the fibre washers.

DISMANTLING NOTES

Removing Pedal Board. This is constructed of two halves, the near-side half being blank and the off-side one slotted to receive the gear lever and foot pedals. Most dismantling work requires only the removal of the off-side board. To remove it take out the mat and remove the four fixing screws. The near-side board can be similarly removed.

Removing Radiator. First drain the radiator by removing the drain plug at the base of the honeycomb block and then disconnect both water hose connections by removing the clips and forcing the hose off the radiator inlet and outlet pipes. Then remove the nut from the front end of the horizontal radiator stay rod (placed under the tank bracket) and also the two bolts securing the radiator brackets to the spring bracket, when the radiator can be lifted off the chassis.

Removing Dummy Radiator. It is necessary first to disconnect from the dash junction box (adjacent to the petrol tank) the wires which are united in one harness and pass through the hole in the side of the radiator shell and then to draw the harness clear of the radiator through this hole. Afterwards slacken the locknut where the stay joins the radiator top and remove the other stay rod nut inside the top of the radiator. The two bolts holding the radiator brackets to the spring bracket should then be removed when the radiator can be lifted clear. In order to remove the stay rod lock the two nuts at the front end together and unscrew the rod from the hexagon lug holding it to the dashboard. To prevent rotation of the lug, grip it with a spanner while doing this.

Removing Swivels. To remove the front wheels complete with swivels and driving shafts is perfectly simple once the track rod connecting the two wheels has been disconnected. Before this can be done, however, it is necessary to remove the spring bolts at the outer ends of the springs (a pair of these are provided per wheel), and slacken the grub screws on each of the flexible couplings.

Gearbox Removal. The radiator and also the swivels must be removed as already described, after which the flexible couplings should be slid out until they clear the differential shafts. Then take off the spring bracket above the differential case. The electric starter and the gearbox cover should then be taken off by removing their securing bolts, and also remove the nut from the stud on the under side of the differential case, and, finally, the bolts holding the gearbox to the clutch chamber should be undone to allow

MAINTENANCE AND OVERHAUL

of the gearbox being slid bodily forward and lifted clear of the chassis.

How to Remove the Engine. It is possible to remove the engine and gearbox together, but it is undoubtedly more convenient to detach the gearbox first as already described. To remove the engine, the carburettor petrol pipe should first be disconnected. During this operation see that the fibre washers on each side of the union are not lost. Then remove the H.T. leads and take off the distributor cap. Also disconnect the small diameter wire on the distributor. Detach the throttle, strangler, and ignition controls from the accelerator bracket on the dashboard if dealing with an air-cooled model (throttle and starter carburettor controls if dealing with a water-cooled model), and withdraw the pin at the forward end of the clutch actuating rod. Finally, disconnect the two dynamo cables and remove the two bolts, one on each side of the engine, which hold it in place on the two chassis frame members, and lift the engine out.

Removing Rear Wheel Arm. If the rear wheel is first removed, it will considerably simplify removal of the wheel arm which can be done in the following manner. Undo the bolts holding the bearing caps in position on the trunnion bracket and disconnect the rear brake either at the brake lever on the brake cover plate or the rocking lever on the trunnion bracket. Then release the shock absorber pressure and draw the arm out to the rear. It will come away together with the rear spring and the "Silentbloc" housing.

Do not Fix Badges on the Radiator Honeycomb. The attachment of badges or similar devices to the radiator honeycomb is very undesirable as this tends to impede the air flow, especially in the case of air-cooled models, and so cause overheating. If it is necessary to attach badges, fix them to some part of the radiator shell, not to the honeycomb itself.

SUMMARY OF ENGINE TROUBLES

Possible engine troubles are many, and include fairly obscure troubles capable of temporarily baffling even an expert, but troubles which can be regarded as reasonably likely to occur are few and capable of rapid diagnosis and cure. A few years ago engine trouble was far more common than it is to-day. Present-day cars are almost 100 per cent reliable, and therefore it is not proposed to enter into a long discussion on engine trouble. A clear summary of the important points to be looked to when trouble occurs is really all that is necessary.

Engine Refuses to Start.

1. If the starter button when pressed causes no engine rotation,

the self-starter system is not functioning. Use the starting handle until the electrical fault (see Chapter VII) can be rectified.

2. If the starter button when pressed does rotate the engine, trouble may be due to faulty petrol supply or ignition.

3. To test for petrol supply, remove the float chamber and note if petrol flows from the needle valve. If it does, there is no shortage of fuel. If starting is still impossible, look for the following ignition faults: (*a*) loose H.T. wires, (*b*) dirty plugs, (*c*) incorrect plug gap (page 33), (*d*) slack contact-breaker arm or incorrectly adjusted points. It is not a bad plan to remove the plug from the cylinder, lay it on top and note for sparking with lead connected and body earthed and engine turned slowly by hand.

4. If the petrol does not flow on removing the float chamber, the trouble may be due to a choked supply, but first be sure the tap is on. Clean petrol filter and blow through pipe until the obstruction is cleared.

Engine Starts but Immediately Stops.

Depress the accelerator pedal gently when the engine starts, advance the ignition (O.H.V. models), and rev the engine up for a few seconds to get it warm, pulling the air strangler or starter carburettor control knob if the engine spits back due to a weak mixture. If the engine will not accelerate, but stalls immediately the accelerator pedal is depressed, the trouble is probably due to dirt or water present in the jets. The jets should be removed and cleaned and all petrol drained from the float chamber.

Engine Misfires or Blows Back into Carburettor.

1. If trouble occurs with a cold engine it may disappear as the engine warms up.

2. If trouble persists with a warm engine, it is probably due to water or dirt in the jets which should be removed and cleaned. Be sure first, however, that the trouble is not due to running on a very excessive ignition advance or to a weak inlet valve spring.

The engine in this case will not tick-over regularly, and on an attempt being made to reduce the revolutions it will probably stall. If at this moment it is found that momentary depression of the float chamber tickler causes the engine to pick up, it is practically a certainty that air leaks are occurring. Good tick-over is quite impossible to obtain if air leaks are present, because whatever adjustments are made the slow-running mixture is incorrect due to the admission of excessive air *via* means other than those allowed for in the design of the carburettor. The

MAINTENANCE AND OVERHAUL 77

only effective remedy is to press out the old valve guides and fit new ones.

Engine Misfires on One or More Cylinders.
1. H.T. lead disconnected at plug or distributor.
2. Sooted, carbonized or cracked plug. Run the engine for a short time and then ascertain which of the plugs is the cooler. This is probably the one at fault. Examine and replace if necessary.
3. Excessively wide plug gaps or unsuitable plug.
4. If none of the above is the cause of misfiring, perhaps a tappet requires adjusting or a valve spring has fractured. The rocker box or valve cover should be removed and the springs examined, particularly the exhaust valve springs.

Engine Stops Suddenly.
1. Ignition trouble should be suspected if there is no warning. Have a look at the distributor.
2. If the stoppage is preceded by spitting back in the carburettor, the petrol supply is probably at fault. Make sure that the tap is on and there is sufficient fuel. Also, look for obstructions in the jets or pipe filters.

Loss of Power.
1. Is handbrake off?
2. Check valve clearances and inspect valve springs.
3. See that the ignition control lever is operating the contact-breaker correctly.
4. Is decarbonizing necessary? Loss of power due to carbon deposits comes on gradually.

Noise or Vibration.
1. Check valve clearances. Excessive clearances produce a persistent clicking.
2. Make sure that the nuts holding rocker cases to the cylinders are tight.
3. See that none of the engine mounting bolts are loose.

If Acceleration is Poor. First assure yourself that the carburettor is properly adjusted. If the performance remains bad although the adjustment is correct, it may be desirable to fit a slightly larger main jet, but, as a rule, the choke tube should not be interfered with. Poor acceleration is sometimes caused by a weak spark due either to a faulty plug or run-down batteries. In the latter case, it is advisable to set the plug points somewhat closer than usual so as to offer slightly less electrical resistance to the passage of a weak spark.

If Acceleration is Impossible. Provided that starting and tickover are possible, complete absence of acceleration under load can only be caused by obstruction of the main jet, a weak magneto, loss of compression, or other engine defects.

Low Maximum Speed. If the mechanical condition of the engine is good, the spark advance is correct, the engine does not need decarbonizing and the tappets are correctly adjusted, it is possible that carburation is at fault. It is advisable, however, to check the spark advance, as sufficient advance is most important to obtain high speed, and also to make sure that the silencer is not choked, which is usually indicated by the absence of a clearly-marked exhaust note at the tail pipe. Possible carburation defects are: (1) Defective petrol supply, (2) butterfly valve not opening fully; (3) too small a main jet (see page 67).

(1) *Defective Petrol Supply.* It is always possible to recognize this, as acceleration is generally satisfactory up to a certain speed, after which periodic backfiring and hesitation occurs, which is remedied by a slight throttle reduction. To confirm matters, remove the float chamber and note the rate of petrol flow from the needle valve.

(2) *Butterfly Not Opening Fully.* The butterfly valve should be wide open when the accelerator pedal is depressed to its fullest extent. To check this, note the position of the limit screw which should be in contact with the boss cast on the outside of the throttle chamber.

Knocking Tendency. Knocking, if due to carburation, can only be caused by a weak mixture, and if it cannot be cured by fitting a main jet one size larger, other causes, such as air leaks, must be looked for. The most prevalent causes are excessive ignition advance, a carbonized engine, dirty plugs. Pre-ignition due to these causes should not be confused with mechanical noises due to worn bearings, slack pistons, etc.

Overheating. Where water cooling is concerned, overheating naturally cannot occur if there is sufficient water in the radiator, and even on air-cooled engines, serious overheating, if it does occur, is seldom traceable to carburation. It is far more likely to be caused by insufficient lubrication. The temperature can certainly be raised to some extent by running on an excessively weak or over-rich mixture or with the spark retarded.

High Fuel Consumption. It should be possible to obtain at least 40 m.p.g. on an air-cooled model, and 40 m.p.g. on a water-cooled model at ordinary cruising speeds, and it is a good plan to make a definite test of the fuel consumption over a known distance on average give-and-take roads. The longer the test the greater will be the accuracy of the reading. Speedometer mileage readings should not be relied upon for the test, neither

MAINTENANCE AND OVERHAUL

should it be taken for granted that a quantity of fuel supplied from a pump is the amount it is supposed to be. The best plan is to drain the fuel tank completely or else use a small auxiliary tank.

High fuel consumption may be brought about through many factors, singly or combined. For instance, habitual fast driving with little throttling down will in itself cause a very thirsty engine. The same applies to the driving of air-cooled models (with variable ignition) with the spark insufficiently advanced. As regards carburation troubles governing high fuel consumption, any factor which results in incomplete combustion does waste fuel considerably. This includes a weak or an excessively rich mixture with or without actual misfiring. Direct fuel wastage due to actual leakage from union joints (page 67) or flooding of the carburettor may be present, or it is possible that the main jet cap is loose or the jet is not for some reason seating correctly in its carrier.

Another feature which controls fuel consumption to a great extent is the mechanical condition of the engine. Any serious frictional losses absorb power and, if compression is bad due to worn piston rings or pitted valves, the power is entirely misdirected, and fuel consumption goes up by leaps and bounds. Troubles of this kind, however, are so apparently noticeable due to the set-back in performance that they rarely pass undetected.

CHAPTER VI

LUBRICATION

IN this chapter I would point out the great importance of keeping your engine correctly lubricated. Not only should the car be regularly lubricated, but the right grade and brand of oil only should be used. Do not be persuaded into buying an oil "just as good" as some well-known make, but insist on one of the brands tabled at the end of this chapter. These oils have been thoroughly tested and are recommended with confidence that they are the most suitable oils for the purpose. Do not, under any circumstances, use one of the former oils; if you do, it may ruin your engine, and the saving of a few shillings will be turned into a loss of several pounds.

During the running-in period it would be advantageous to use one of the grades of upper cylinder lubricant now on the market. The addition of the correct amount of one of these to the petrol reduces the tendency towards seizure with a new engine if it is overdriven. When the engine has been well run-in, however, it is unlikely that the upper cylinder lubricant will be of appreciable benefit, and it is still less likely to be of value with old or badly-worn engines.

Special attention has been paid to the designing of the Three Wheeler to the reduction of the number of parts which require lubrication, with a view to reducing, as far as possible, the time required to attend to it. The engine, gearbox, clutch, and differential are lubricated automatically, so that it is only necessary to replenish the supply of oil at frequent intervals, while the remaining parts are dealt with by the grease-gun system.

DESCRIPTION OF THE LUBRICATION SYSTEM

Twin-cylinder Models. As already stated, the engine is automatically lubricated by a rotary gear pump which is driven through spiral gears by the crankshaft. The pump is, therefore, always in operation when the engine is running. The lower portion of the crankcase casting forms an oil sump, which, when full, contains sufficient oil for several hundred miles. From the sump the pump draws oil through the filter C (Figs. 46 and 47) and then forces it up the vertical pipe D. At E there is a small branch pipe which projects a spray of oil on to the timing gears and their bearings. The main oil supply then passes through the adjustable control valve F and through two branch pipes which

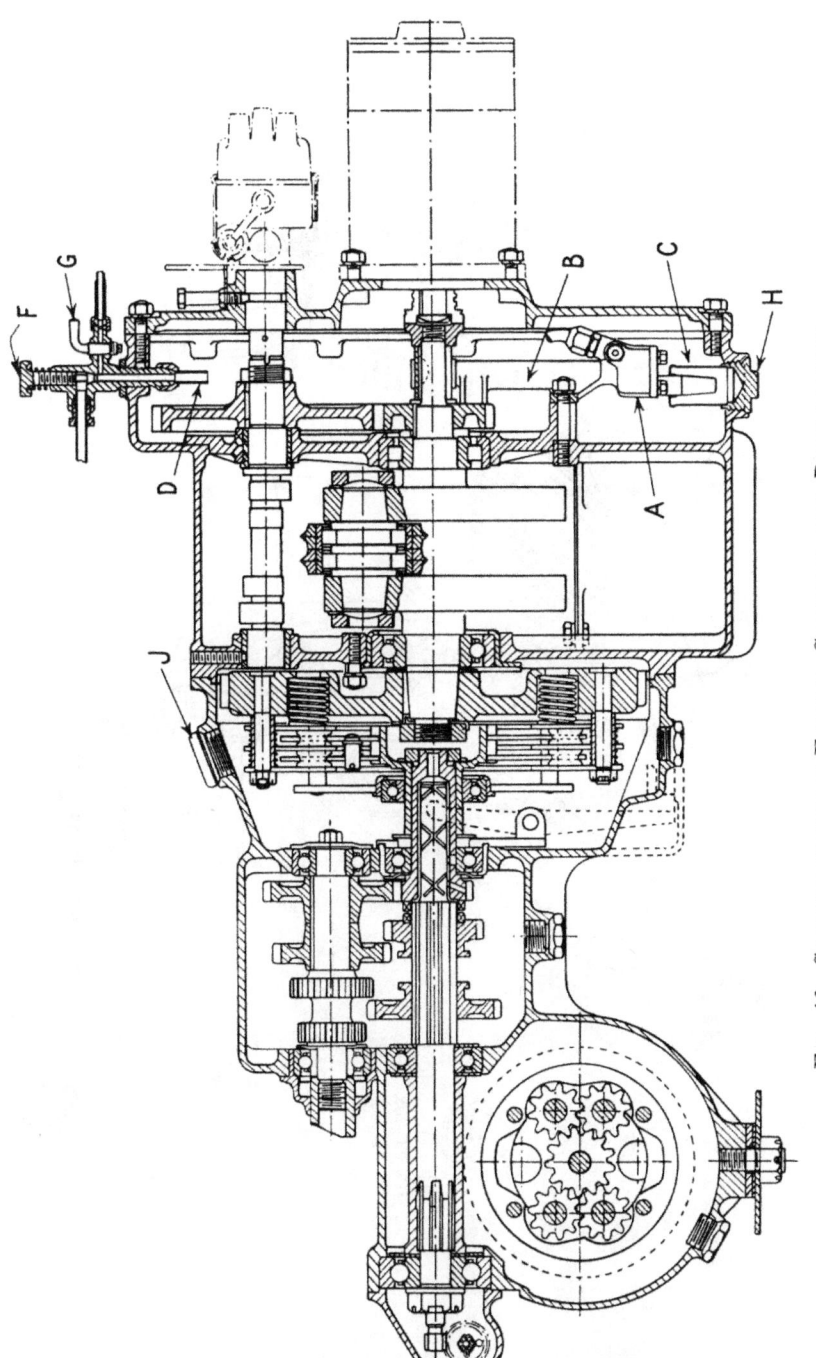

Fig. 46. Section through Engine, Gearbox, and Differential
(Air-cooled models.)

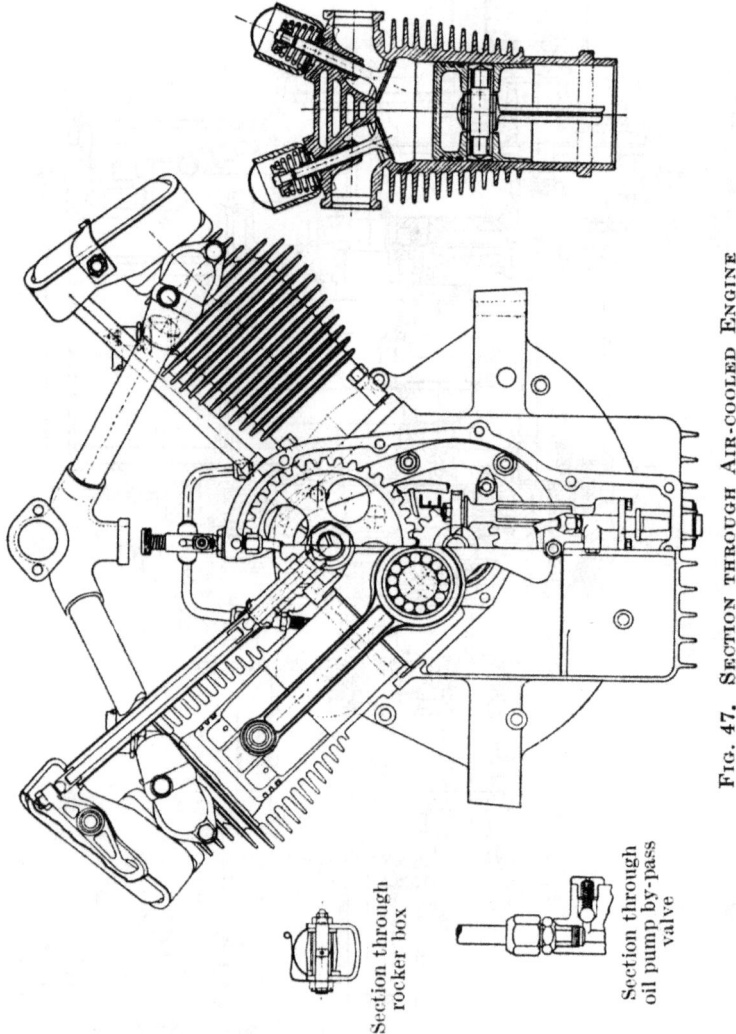

Fig. 47. Section through Air-cooled Engine

Section through rocker box

Section through oil pump by-pass valve

go to the base of each cylinder. (The valve F is fitted with a safety device which prevents it from being shut right off.) At the top of the timing case a branch pipe connected to the main oil pipe communicates through the cock G with the oil-pressure gauge on the instrument panel. Each piston, therefore, picks up the oil each time it reaches the bottom of its stroke, and is thus positively lubricated. The surplus oil drops down on to the crankshaft and big ends, which are, of course, rotating, and is thus splashed over the main and big-end bearings. The gudgeon pins are similarly lubricated by this splash, as are the camshaft and cams.

The overhead valve gear on each cylinder is lubricated in the following manner. As the pistons descend they cause a certain amount of pressure in the crankcase, tending to force the air out. This air, which is heavily charged with oil through the splashing action of the crankshaft, can only escape through breather grooves cut in the four tappet guides. Since the tubes which surround the push rods form an air-tight passage between the tappet guides and the overhead valve rocker boxes, it is evident that the oil-charged air which is forced out of the crankcase through the tappet guides at each revolution of the engine must pass up these tubes into the valve rocker boxes, where it is absorbed by felt washers fixed to the rockers and thus provides lubrication for the bearings. It is advisable, however, periodically to lubricate the upper ends of the push rods and also the felt washers with an oil can. In passing through the tubes and rocker cases the air deposits oil on all the moving parts, which are thus kept well lubricated. When overhauling, note that a hardened steel washer is fitted to the inner side of each rocker pin, and that this must be replaced in this position in order to take the thrust. Grease-gun nipples are also fitted to the rocker pins. These should be lubricated regularly (every 150–200 miles).

The oil pressure gauge referred to previously shows the oil pressure in the lubrication system while the engine is running. The actual reading depends upon the temperature of the engine and the nature of the oil used. With a cold engine and a thick oil a high pressure will be shown, while a hot engine or thin oil will give a lower reading. For normal running the pressure should be between 2 lb. and 6 lb. per sq. in. If the pressure falls much below 2 lb. it is an indication either that the supply of oil in the sump is nearly exhausted, or that the filter C, Fig. 46, has become clogged and requires cleaning, or that the oil is in such a dirty condition that it should be replaced with a fresh supply.

Four-cylinder Models. As on the air-cooled models, the engine is automatically lubricated by a rotary gear pump A, Fig. 48, at the lower end of vertical shaft B which is driven through spiral

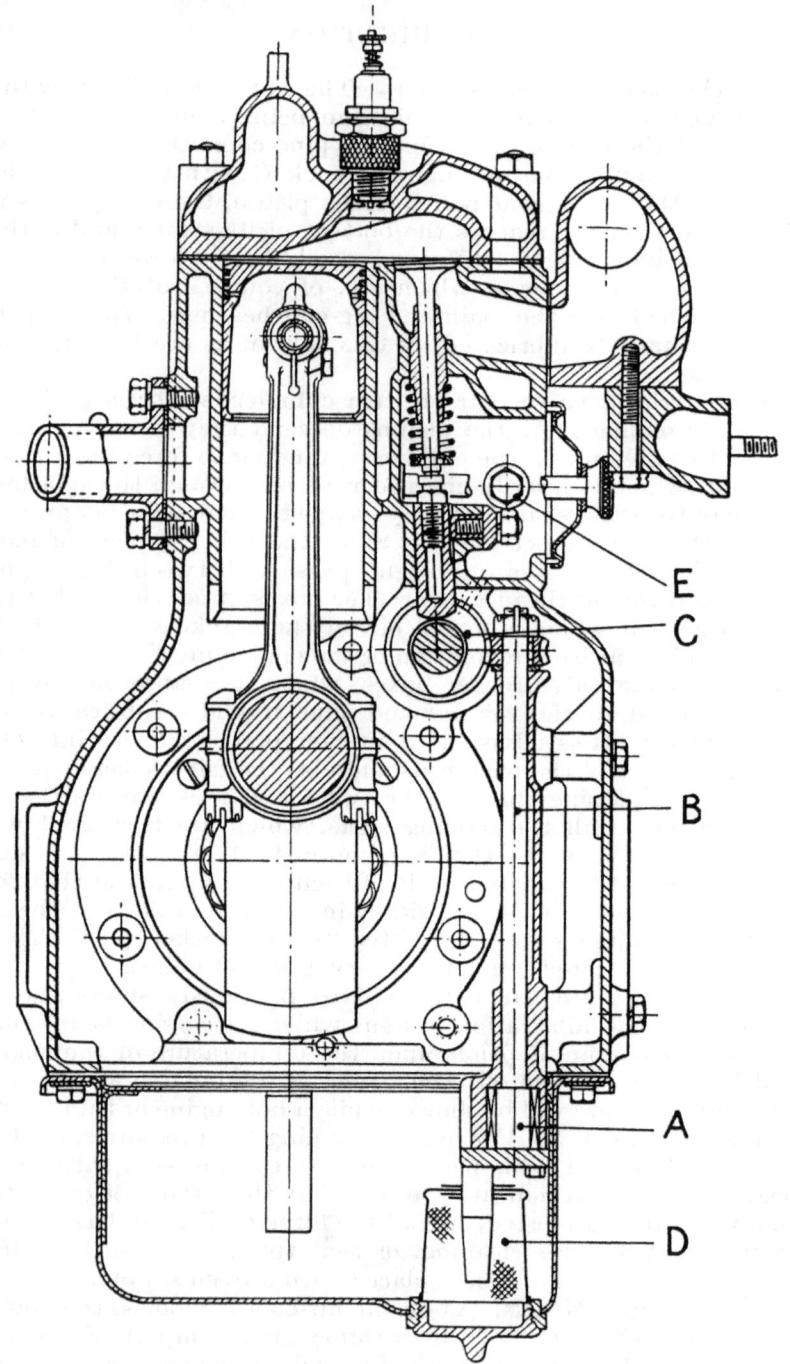

Fig. 48. Lubrication Details of the Four-cylinder Engine

gears from the camshaft at *C*. An extension on the pump body projects into the engine sump, the capacity of which is 1 gal. In operation, the pump draws oil through filter *D* in the sump and delivers it under pressure through a channel drilled in the cylinder block to the timing case, where a portion of it is diverted through a specially calibrated orifice to the tappet chest at *E*. At this point a well is formed which fills up with oil and from which the oil drains through holes in the tappet guides and then passes to the camshaft. Any excess of oil in the well returns to the sump through two drain holes placed at the correct level, one at each end of the tappet chest.

The main oil supply, part of which is diverted to the tappets and cams as described above, passes through a passage in the timing cover to a special union *F*, through which it is forced to the hollow crankshaft, emerging through a hole drilled in each of the crankshaft journals and thus lubricating the big-end bearings. The pistons, cylinders, and small-end bearings are lubricated by splash.

An oil-pressure gauge is mounted in the instrument panel. Under normal conditions when the engine is warm the pressure gauge should read about 60 lb. per square inch. At low engine speeds the pressure reading may fall somewhat, but so long as there is an adequate supply of oil in the engine sump the pressure should be maintained when the engine is running.

At *G* (Fig. 49) a spring-loaded relief valve is fitted to the pump. If the oil-pressure gauge does not show a normal pressure it is either due to shortage of oil in the sump or the valve not seating properly. Pull out the dipstick on the near side of the engine and examine the oil level. If this is in order, replace the dipstick and check the relief valve.

This valve has been designed in such a way that it can be cleaned of dirt or other obstructions. To clean the valve leave the engine ticking over, take hold of the small projection (see Fig. 49) and pull it outwards, releasing it after a second or two. In addition to this, if necessary, rotate the valve slowly in order to assist the removal of the obstruction.

There is no adjustable control in the B.S.A. lubrication system, and the only points requiring attention are a periodical examination of the oil level in the sump and a careful check on the oil-pressure reading in the gauge.

After many thousands of miles the oil pressure may fall on account of wear developing at the connecting rod big-end bearings.

Oil Level. It is necessary for the owner to make sure that there is always sufficient oil in the sump, remembering that when full it contains sufficient for a considerable mileage. Nevertheless,

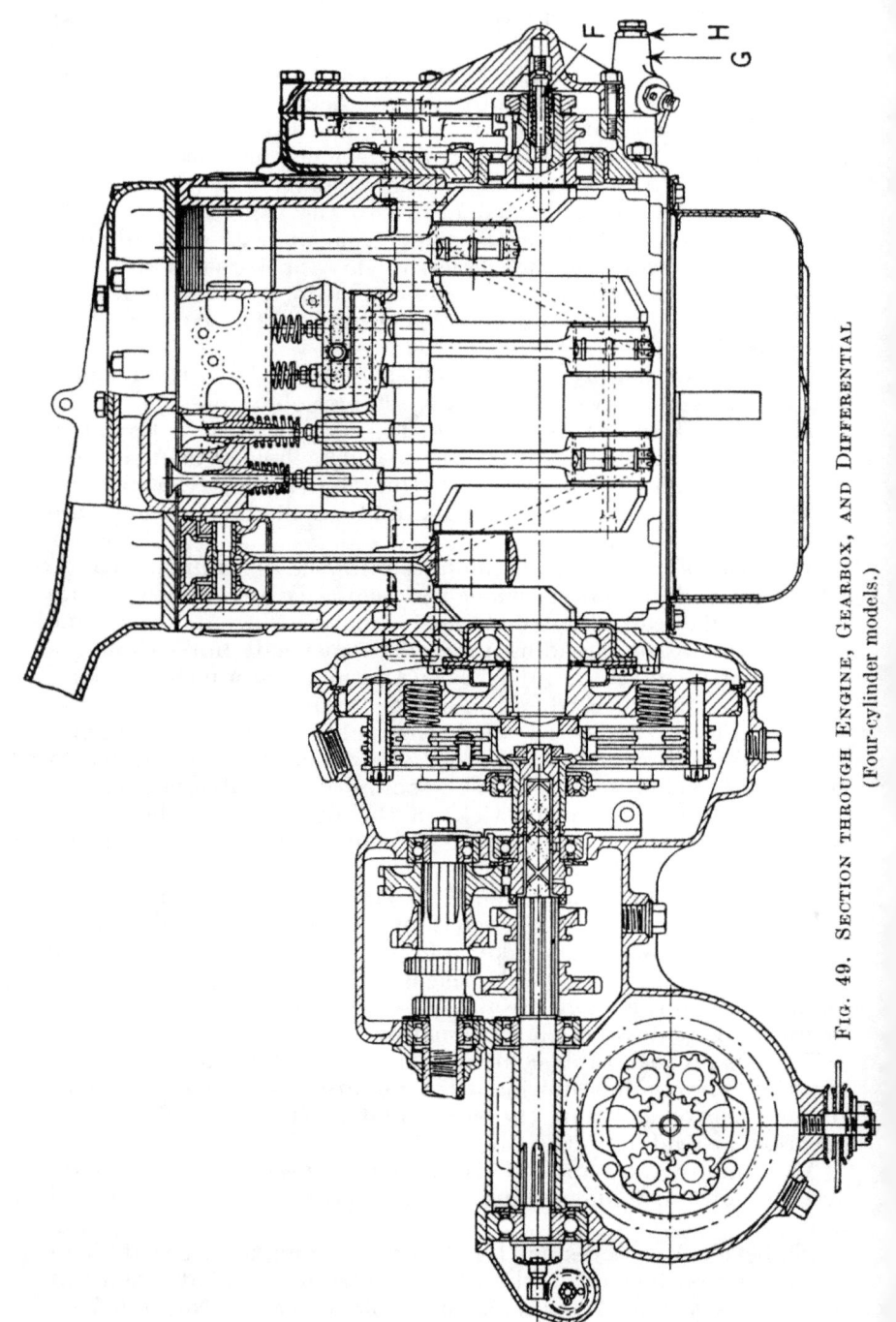

FIG. 49. SECTION THROUGH ENGINE, GEARBOX, AND DIFFERENTIAL.
(Four-cylinder models.)

LUBRICATION

the owner should make a regular habit of withdrawing the oil-level dipstick every morning and examining it. In the case of the air-cooled models it is marked off to show the level to which the oil should be poured in. No journey should be commenced with the sump less than half full, however short the journey may be, and it is preferable to top up the sump every morning. Note that the sump filler cap should not be removed while the engine is running.

The oil level on the four-cylinder models is shown by the dipstick on the nearside of the crankcase. The dipstick is marked F for full and "1" when 1 qt. is required, "2" when 2 qt. are required to replenish the sump. The oil level should never be allowed to fall as low as the "2" mark. The oil sump should be drained and refilled with fresh oil after the first 500 miles and then after every 2,000 miles.

Clutch. The clutch requires a little oil occasionally, which should be poured in through the filler hole J (Fig. 46). If a $\frac{1}{4}$ pt. of engine oil (see above) is put in every 500 miles it will be sufficient. Apart from this the clutch will require no attention. Do not let the clutch run without oil. If the filler cap is removed while the engine is running, a considerable film of oil should be visible on the fly-wheel. If the fly-wheel appears dry, stop the engine and pour oil in the clutch chamber as instructed above until a film appears on the fly-wheel when the engine is running. There will then be sufficient oil in the clutch chamber, and the filler cap may be replaced.

Gearbox. The gearbox should be replenished through the filling orifice every 1,000 miles. For this purpose the following oils are recommended: Castrol D, Mobiloil C, or Speedwell Crimsangere Light.

Before adding oil to the gearbox remove the level plug provided on the near-side of the box. Add only sufficient WARM oil to bring the level to this plug hole. Failure to observe this instruction may result in difficult starting, overheating, and seizure.

To fill an empty gearbox about 1 pt. of oil is required.

Every 2,000 miles flush out the gearbox with paraffin, after draining out all the old oil by removing the drain plug in the bottom. Replace the drain plug and refill with fresh oil up to the correct level. These operations are carried out more easily when the gearbox is warm, i.e. immediately after a run.

Differential. To lubricate the differential it is necessary to remove the front number plate by unscrewing the four nuts which hold it in position. Behind the number plate a filler plug will be seen. Remove this and pour in oil until it reaches the level of the filler plug. Lubrication of the differential is quite automatic, providing the oil level is maintained. If the oil level is too high there is a danger of oil reaching the brake linings.

It will be found much easier to get the oil to flow in if the refilling is done when the car has just come in from a long run, as the gears will be warm and so the oil will flow more easily. If the oil flows in slowly, jack up one of the front wheels and turn the wheel forwards by hand while the oil is being poured in. The oil should be warmed before pouring in. The forward motion of the worm wheel will then tend to draw the oil in. If at any time there is any doubt as to the amount of oil in the differential case, due to the thick oil being so sluggish as not to show the proper level, drain all the oil out through the drain plug, and then put in $1\frac{1}{2}$ pt. of oil.

With a new car it will be advisable to drain the oil out and refill with the quantity mentioned above when the car has covered 200 miles. When replacing the filler cap remember to screw it up tightly. Be very careful what oil is used in the differential, as an unsuitable oil might cause damage to the worm gear by which the front axle is driven. The same grades of oils as recommended for the gearbox (see page 87) should be used in the differential. After prolonged running a slight "weep" of oil may be observed on the differential and cap, but this is quite in order.

Miscellaneous Parts. All other parts of the chassis which require lubrication can be supplied with grease by means of the grease-gun which is supplied in the tool kit.

To lubricate, place the nozzle of the gun to the nipple and by pushing the handle of the gun down several times, grease will be forced into the working parts at high pressure; continue this operation until the grease exudes from the joint faces.

Figs. 50 and 51 show the positions of all the nipples to which the grease-gun should be applied. It cannot be too strongly stated that the few minutes required to inject grease at all these points once a week will be time well spent. The improvement in the general smoothness in running will alone amply repay the trouble taken, while the reduction in maintenance costs resulting will undoubtedly be appreciable.

Grease nipples are provided for the front hubs, but the rear hub is lubricated by filling the hub cap with grease and screwing it in position.

It will also be found that 5 minutes' work with the grease-gun immediately after the car has come in from a long run through heavy rain or on very wet roads will be well worth while. The action of forcing grease into the bearings automatically forces out any water or dirt which may have entered, and this prevents such parts as the steering joints or spring bearings from rusting or becoming stiff. Use only good quality grease, as poor grease will go hard and block up the passages through which it has to

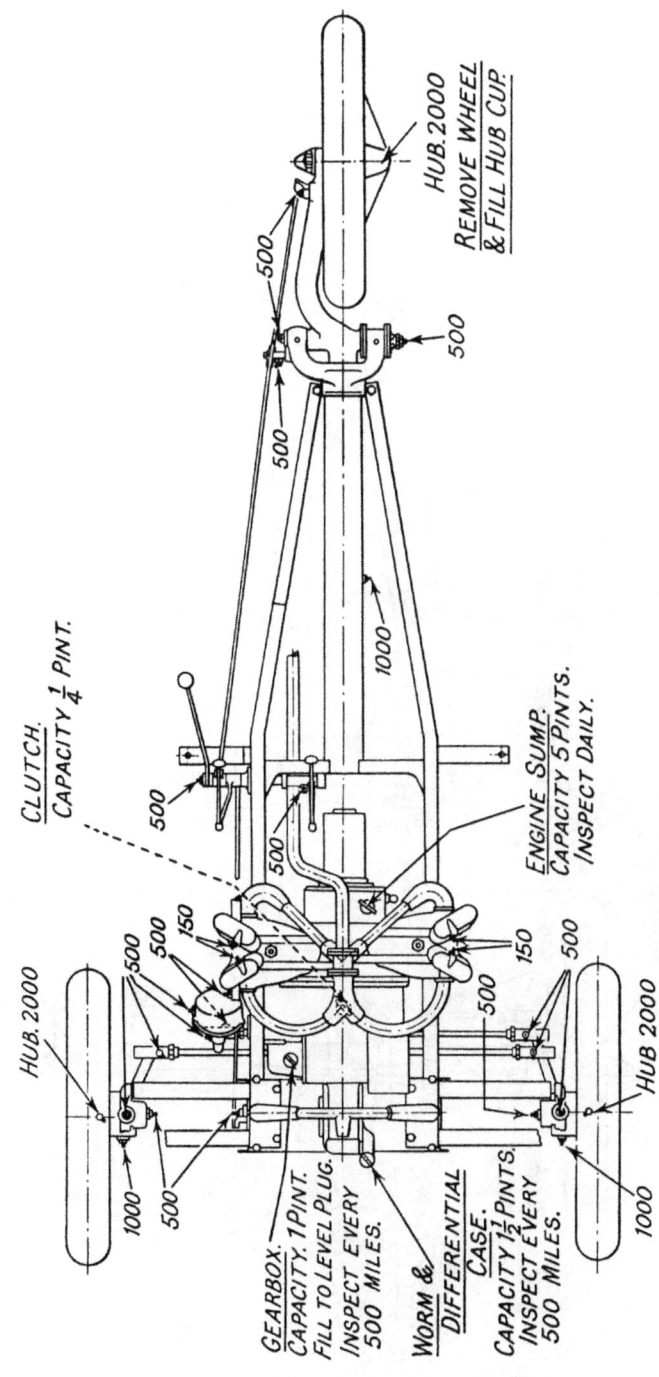

Fig. 50. Lubrication Chart of the Air-cooled Models

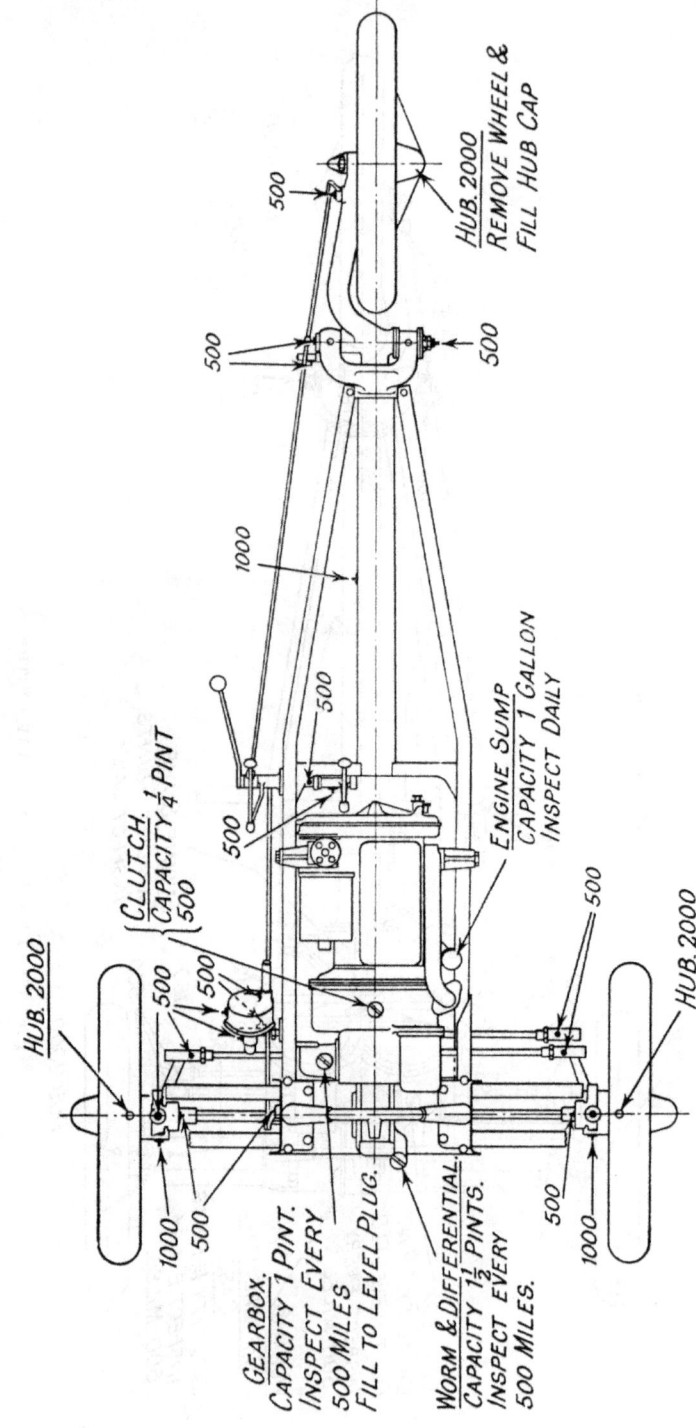

Fig. 51. Lubrication Chart of the Four-cylinder Models

LUBRICATION

pass, while it may contain acid matter, which will corrode the highly-finished bearing surfaces.

Put a few spots of oil on the carburettor and ignition (air-cooled models only) control rod joints occasionally, and also on the fork joints on the brake gear to prevent them becoming stiff.

Springs. All the springs are thoroughly greased before the car leaves the factory. It is advisable, however, to re-grease the front springs every six months. The spring leaves should be separated by means of a small wedge and grease introduced between them with an old knife. This attention will ensure good springing and perfect comfort on bad road surfaces throughout the life of the car. Be careful to use a grease which will not go hard at low temperatures or after long periods of use. In the case of the rear spring, which is enclosed within the rear frame member, this should only require regreasing at very infrequent intervals, say, every time the car is overhauled.

Engine Oil. The following brands of lubricating oil are recommended for the Three Wheeler—

	Air-cooled Model		Water-cooled Model	
	Summer	Winter	Summer	Winter
Castrol	XL	AA	XL	AA
Vacuum Mobiloil	D	D	BB	AF
Speedwell	SE	SE	SEZ	SEZ

To obtain the most satisfactory service from the car it is essential to use only high quality lubricants—this point cannot be over-emphasized. It is also most important that only one of the above oils should be used, also make sure you are receiving the correct grade.

After every 2,000 miles the sump should be drained. This should always be done when the engine is hot, i.e. immediately after a run, as the old oil will come away much cleaner (or, more strictly, dirtier) than it would if it were cold. Paraffin should not be used as it sometimes loosens deposits without removing them and may cause trouble later in the form of choked oil-ways, etc.

CHAPTER VII

THE ELECTRICAL EQUIPMENT
LIGHTING AND STARTING

THE electrical equipment of the B.S.A. consists of a dynamo which is driven by the engine, the starter motor, the battery, lamps and the necessary wiring. The function of the dynamo is to supply the current for the operation of these fitments; it also supplies current for the operation of the ignition system which is described on page 95. The output from the dynamo is controlled by what is known as the third brush method. This method is used to regulate the output of the dynamo at high speeds and to keep it steady irrespective of the speed at which the dynamo is running. The dynamo speed, of course, must vary because it is driven by the engine. The dynamo is arranged to give alternative outputs. For instance, when running in daylight half charge can be used. This rate is only to be used in the summer when the lights are in little demand. The full charge must be used in the winter when the lights are in much greater demand. This arrangement allows you to keep the battery in good condition always. Between the dynamo and the battery is the cut-out. This is in effect an automatic switch which acts as a valve in the dynamo charging circuit, allowing a flow of current from the dynamo to the battery only. It completes the charging circuit when the dynamo is running fast enough to generate a voltage sufficiently high to charge the battery and disconnects it again when the speed is low. It is not generally known that the cut-out serves no other purpose than that of preventing current from flowing from the battery through the dynamo windings when the car is running slowly or when it is stationary. It does not prevent overcharging of the battery, as many people think.

We will now run over the circuit in order that we may see what takes place when the equipment is in use. When we switch on we allow current to flow to the coil for the purpose of ignition. Then we operate the starter switch, and this allows current to flow and operate the starter motor. When the engine is running it is of course driving the dynamo, but no charging of the battery takes place until the cut-out operates. When the engine speed is increased the cut-out will operate and allow current to pass to the battery. You can observe the cut-out coming into operation by watching the ammeter on the dashboard. You will notice that as the speed of the engine is increased the needle will flicker over to the charge side, the flicker indicating that the cut-out has operated. As the speed of the engine is further increased the needle will rise until it reaches maximum charging rate and will remain nearly constant, irrespective of the car speed, owing to the third brush regulating system. When the car is in use at night with lights on, current flows from the battery to the lamps. If the lamps are on when the car is stationary and engine not running, all current for lighting has to come from the battery and the amount will be shown on the discharge side of the ammeter. When you are running with lights on, the ammeter will show the difference of the amount of current being discharged by the battery, and the current passing to the battery from the dynamo, e.g. the charging rate is 6 amp., while the lights are taking 3 amp. The ammeter will show 5 amp. on the charge side. When you stop the car the cut-out will operate and a discharge of 3 amp. will be shown.

Now let us deal with the maintenance of the equipment. First the dynamo, which is situated on the platform at the front end of the engine. This really requires very little attention, but periodical inspection is recommended.

Brushes. To gain access to the brushes slacken the single screw from the metal cover; this will allow the cover to be taken away. Be careful not to lose the nut as the cover is liable to fly open when the screw is released. Test the action of the brush holders and see that they have sufficient spring tension to hold the brushes firmly pressed against the commutator when the dynamo is running. They should also be free to move on their pivots. This is about all that can be done to the brushes by the owner-driver. After long use the brushes will become so worn that new ones will be necessary; do not try to do this job yourself but rather go to a Lucas Service Depot, in order that the necessary job of bedding down can be done properly.

The Commutator. The commutator upon which the brushes press will need cleaning at intervals in order to keep it free from oil and dust from the brushes. If the car is in regular use this should be done about once a month. Do not neglect this job as dirt will cause sparking at the brushes, which will have the effect of shortening the life of the dynamo. It is a very easy matter to clean; all that is needed is a clean duster and a piece of suitably shaped wood. Stretch the duster over the end of the wood and hold it against the commutator, slowly revolving the armature as you do so. Make sure that the segments or slots in the commutator are quite clean and free from dust. If they are not, clean them out by using part of an old hacksaw blade. Do not exert too much pressure when doing this for fear of damaging the material in the segments.

Field Fuse. This needs little explanation, as I believe that most owners will know that fuses are really a form of safety valve which will break the circuit should any fault occur and so save considerable damage to the equipment. A fuse in the dynamo field circuit will be found together with the half-charge resistance in a small rectangular unit fixed on the dynamo yoke. The fuse is of the cartridge type. If it is found that the dynamo is failing to charge (this is indicated by the ammeter showing a discharge during daytime running) the fuse should be inspected. If it is found that the fuse has blown, examine the charging circuit wiring for a loose or broken connection, and remedy. Fit the replacement fuse provided. Should it blow again after the engine has been started I advise you to take the car to a service station, as the trouble may be serious. Replacement fuses are of the 6-amp. type, and no attempt should be made to use any other type or value.

Lubrication. The only lubrication necessary is a few drops of oil every 1,000 miles, introduced in the lubricator at either end of the dynamo. The bearings are packed with grease on leaving the works. They will need repacking after 5,000 miles have been covered, and you will be well advised to have this done at a service station, as the treatment is of a special nature.

STARTER MOTOR

The armature spindle of the starter motor is fitted with a pinion which engages with a geared ring integral with the fly-wheel of the engine. The pinion is absolutely automatic in action. When the starter switch is operated the pinion engages with the fly-wheel. When the engine starts the pinion returns to its original position. Should it be found that the pinion does not engage, examine the screwed sleeve on the shaft to make sure that it is free from dirt. If necessary, clean with paraffin and give a few drops of thin oil. Very rarely the starter pinion becomes jammed in mesh. Should this happen it is easily freed by removing the metal cap (Fig. 52) at the end of the starter motor and turning the squared end of the shaft with a spanner. The commutator and brushes should be kept clean in the same manner as the dynamo. It will amply repay you to exercise some thought in the use of your starter. Do not try starting your engine on a cold morning without first giving a few turns with the starting handle; this will free the pistons in the cylinders and thus make it easier for the starter to turn the engine. The engine should be switched off when turning the engine by hand. Do not forget to switch on again when you use the starter.

THE ELECTRICAL EQUIPMENT

A few things to observe when starting the engine—
1. Always retard the ignition (this applies only to the air-cooled model). This minimizes the possibility of back-firing.
2. Operate the starter switch firmly without hesitation.
3. Never operate the starter when the engine is running. If the engine does not fire at once, allow it to come to rest before operating the switch again.

Maintenance of Coil Ignition System, and Lighting System. In the following paragraphs is given the information which I con-

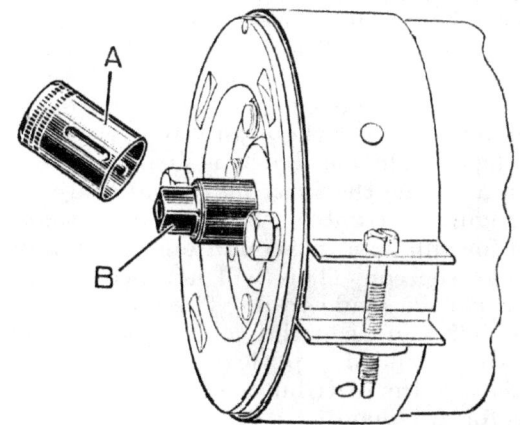

Fig. 52. Squared End of Starter Shaft with Cover Removed

sider necessary for the satisfactory maintenance of the ignition system, together with a brief explanation of how it works.

Current from the battery is passed to the coil which consists of an iron core around which are wound the primary or low tension and the secondary or high tension windings, and it is the function of the coil to convert the battery voltage of 6 volts to a voltage somewhere in the region of 6,000 volts which is necessary to form a spark across the plug points. When you switch on the ignition, current flows from the battery through the primary winding. This current is interrupted by means of the contact-breaker, which causes a high voltage to be induced in the secondary winding. The distributor moulding is provided on the inside with metal inserts, which are in contact with the high tension cables which connect to the sparking plugs. The centre terminal of the distributor moulding is connected on the outside to the high tension terminal on the coil and on the inside it is connected by means of a carbon brush contact to the rotating distributor arm. This arm is provided at its outer tip with a metal electrode, which, when the arm rotates, passes very close to the metal inserts. So the cycle of events is as follows—

When the starter switch is operated the distributor shaft rotates, causing the contact-breaker points to make and break alternately. This causes, every time the points open, a high secondary voltage, which will be passed from the coil to the distributor arm. From here it jumps the gap to one of the metal inserts in the distributor moulding, which in turn is connected by cable to the sparking plug. Immediately after the spark occurs, the contact-breaker points will close and the cycle of operations will be repeated for the spark to occur in the cylinder next in firing order. Very little attention is needed to keep the ignition system in good condition. We will run over all the points which I advise you to give periodical inspection. I am strongly in favour of doing these jobs at fairly regular intervals, as experience has taught me that it is far better to spend time in the comfort of a garage than having to make adjustments on the road through ignition trouble. I have found that these things generally wait for unfavourable conditions to manifest themselves.

First, there is the coil. This will not need to be touched as no adjustment can be made to it. The only advice that can be given here is that you keep the connection terminal clean and tight. Keep the moulded top clean and free from dirt or oil. At intervals remove the distributor moulding (Fig. 16). Examine the electrodes for any deposit; if they are at all dirty, clean them with a cloth which has been damped with petrol. Wipe the distributor with a clean dry rag. Examine the carbon brush and make sure that it slides freely in its holder. Clean the outside of the moulding, paying particular attention to the spaces between the terminals. Now examine the contact-breaker points, and here it is very important that the contacts are kept free from any grease or oil. If they are burned or blackened they may be cleaned with very fine emery cloth, and after with a cloth moistened with petrol. Take special care to see that all particles of dirt and metal dust are wiped away. Failure to keep the contacts clean will result in misfiring.

The contact-breaker gap is carefully set before leaving the works, and a gauge is provided on the spanner dispatched with each distributor. To test the gap, slowly turn the engine over by hand until the contacts are seen to be fully opened. Now insert the gauge on the spanner in the gap; if it is correct the gauge should be a sliding fit. It is not advisable to alter the setting unless the gap varies considerably from the gauge. If adjustment is necessary, proceed as follows—

When the contacts are fully opened, slacken the locking nut "D" on the stationary contact screw, and rotate it by its hexagon head until the gap is set to the thickness of the gauge. After making the adjustment, care must be taken to tighten the locking nut.

Lubrication of Distributor. The main bearing of the distributor on the two-cylinder models is lubricated from a greaser; this should be filled with a good quality grease, and should be given one turn about every 500 miles. On the four-cylinder models,

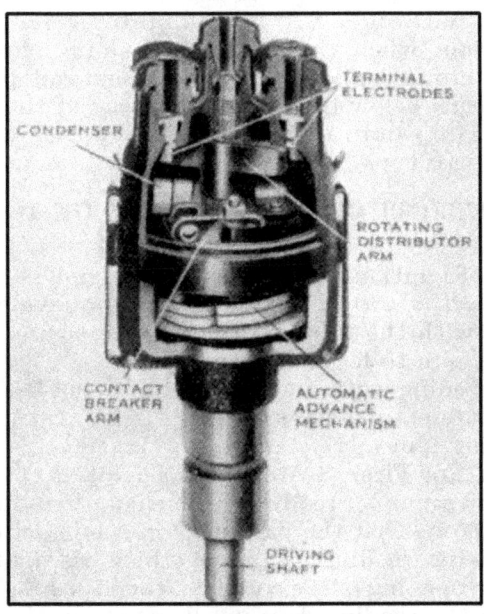

Fig. 53. Typical Distributor with Automatic Advance Mechanism

an oiler is fitted; this should be given one or two drops of oil every 1,000 miles. The cam should be given the slightest smear of vaseline about every 3,000 miles or whenever it appears dry. The pivot J of the contact-breaker should be given a single drop of oil about every 5,000 miles. About every 3,000 miles lift off the rotating distributor arm and add a few drops of thin machine oil. (This applies to the four-cylinder models only.) This is all the lubrication necessary to the ignition system.

Before passing on to the detection and remedy of ignition faults you would be well advised to examine the high tension cables from time to time in order to be sure that they are not perished or cracked. If you find the cables faulty replace them at once, using 7-mm. high tension cable for the purpose; the method of renewing is as follows—

Thread the knurled moulded nut over the cable, bare the end of the cable for about $\frac{1}{4}$ in. and thread the wire through the brass washer and bend back the strands over the side of the washer. Then screw the nut into its terminal.

Ignition Warning Lamp. As already stated, this lamp is incorporated in the instrument panel. It automatically gives a red light whenever the ignition is switched on and the engine is stationary, and so reminds you to switch off. This reduces the possibility of the battery being discharged by current flowing through the coil windings. It will also be noticed that the light will remain when the engine is running slowly. This is because the lamp is connected across the cut-out points and will light up at speeds below the cutting-in speed of the dynamo.

Should the lamp burn out at any time replace with a 2·5-volt ·2-amp. screw-cap type.

THE DETECTION AND REMEDY OF IGNITION FAULTS

If a failure of ignition or misfiring occurs, unless the cause is at once apparent, the owner is strongly recommended to proceed in accordance with the table on the page opposite, which should quickly enable him to locate the trouble.

Before proceeding with the examination, make sure that the trouble is not due to defects in the engine, carburettor, petrol supply, sparking plugs, etc.

Engine Will Not Fire. Switch on the ignition, turn the engine and observe the ammeter reading. The engine should be turned by hand if it is known that the battery is in a low state of charge.

If an ammeter reading is given which rises and falls with the closing and opening of the contacts, then the low tension wiring is in order. If the reading does not fluctuate in this way, a short in the low tension wiring is indicated, or the contacts are remaining open. When no reading is given, a broken or loose connection in the low tension wiring is indicated, or the battery may be exhausted.

If a fault is indicated in the low tension wiring, examine the cables from switch or junction box to coil, and from coil to distributor. See that the battery terminals are tight and that the cables from the switch-box to the battery are secure. The battery may be dismissed as the cause of the trouble if the lamps will light.

Examine the high tension cables, i.e. cables from the coil to the distributor, and from the distributor to the plugs. If the rubber shows signs of deterioration or cracking, the cable should be renewed. Remove the distributor moulding and examine the contacts; if necessary, clean them as described. Turn the engine over by hand and see that the contacts come together.

Test the coil independently of the distributor as follows: remove the cable from the centre distributor terminal, and hold

HOW TO LOCATE AND REMEDY IGNITION TROUBLE

Condition	Method of Detection of Possible Causes	Remedy
Engine will not fire.	Starter will not turn engine and lamps do not give good light. Battery discharged.	Start engine by hand. Battery should be recharged by running car for a long period during daytime with charging switch in full-charge position. Alternatively recharge from an independent electrical supply.
	Controls not set correctly for starting.	See that ignition is switched on, petrol turned on and everything is in order for starting.
	Remove lead from centre distributor terminal and hold it about ¼ in. away from some metal part of the chassis, while engine is turned over. If sparks jump gap regularly, the coil and distributor are functioning correctly. If the coil does not spark, the trouble may be due to any of the following causes—	Examine the sparking plugs, and if these are clean and the gaps correct, the trouble is due to carburettor, petrol supply, etc.
	Fault in low tension wiring. Indicated by (1) No ammeter reading when engine is slowly turned and ignition switch is on, or (2) No spark occurs between the contact points when quickly separated by the fingers when the ignition switch is on.	Examine all cables in ignition circuit, and see that all connections are tight. See that battery terminals are secure.
	Dirty or pitted contact points.	Clean with fine emery cloth and afterwards with a cloth moistened with petrol.
	Contact-breaker points out of adjustment. Turn engine until contacts are fully opened and test gap with gauge on spanner.	Adjust gap to gauge.
Engine misfires.	Dirty or pitted contact points.	Clean with fine emery cloth and afterwards with a cloth moistened with petrol.
	Contact-breaker points out of adjustment. Turn engine until contacts are fully opened and test gap with gauge on spanner.	Adjust gap to gauge.
	Remove each sparking plug in turn, rest it on the cylinder head, and observe whether a spark occurs at the points when the engine is turned. Irregular sparking may be due to dirty plugs or defective high tension cables. If sparking is regular at all plugs the trouble is probably due to engine defects.	Clean plugs and adjust the gaps to ·030 in. (air-cooled model) and ·018 in. (water-cooled model). Replace any lead if the insulation shows signs of deterioration or cracking. Examine carburettor, petrol supply, etc.

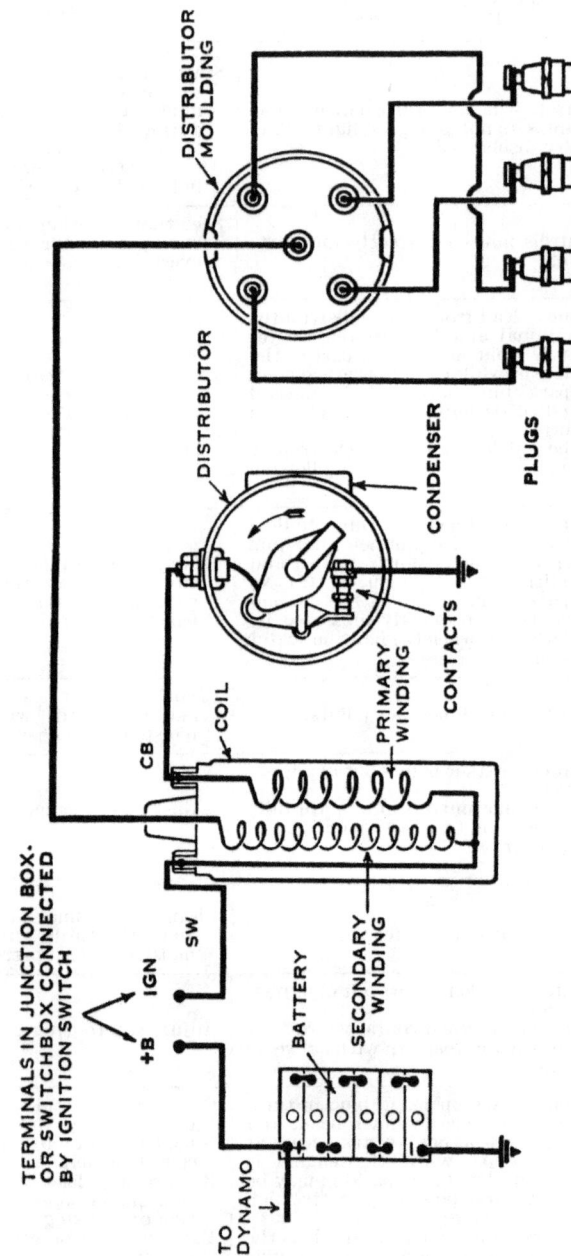

Fig. 54. Coil Ignition Wiring Diagram

THE ELECTRICAL EQUIPMENT 101

it about ¼ in. from some metal part of the chassis and turn the engine. The sparking should be strong and regular if the coil is functioning correctly.

Misfiring and Bad Starting. Examine the high tension cables and the plugs. If necessary, adjust the gaps to the correct setting—about ·030 in. (air-cooled model) and ·018 in. (water-cooled model). Sooty or oiled plugs may be dismantled and washed out with petrol.

The plugs and high tension cables may be tested by removing the plugs in turn and allowing them to rest on the cylinder head and observing whether a spark occurs at the points when the engine is turned by hand. It should, however, be noted that this is only a rough test, since it is possible that a spark may not take place when the plug is under compression.

Remove the distributor moulding and see that the electrodes and contacts are clean. If necessary, clean them as previously described. See that the contact gap setting is correct.

If, after carrying out the examination suggested, the cause of the trouble cannot be found, the equipment should be examined by the nearest service depot.

CARE OF THE LIGHTING SYSTEM

Headlamps. I would stress the importance of having the lamps correctly adjusted and focused, and the occasional checking of this is advised. If the lamps are correctly alined the normal driving beam should be parallel with the road and with each other, in other words, straight ahead. If the lamps become out of alinement or out of focus it has the effect of destroying the anti-dazzle properties. Alinement is very easy; the mountings are universal and are locked by a single nut, and focusing can be carried out by moving the bulb holder backwards and forwards when the clamping clip at the back of the reflector is slackened. Care must be taken to tighten the clip after the adjustment. The important thing to remember is when replacing bulbs use only the bulb specified by the makers. They are specially made to ensure that the filaments will focus accurately with the reflectors. To remove the front of the headlamp, slacken the fixing screw at the bottom of the lamp and swing it aside from the slot. The front can then be withdrawn. When replacing, press the front on to the lamp body, locating the top of the rims first, then swing the screw into the slot and lock the front into position. Should it be found necessary to remove the reflector, turn back the two ends of the cork washer at the top of the rim and withdraw the screw which can then be seen. Do not attempt to clean the reflectors with anything else but a soft chamois leather, as the surfaces are protected with a colourless coating. *On no account use metal polish.*

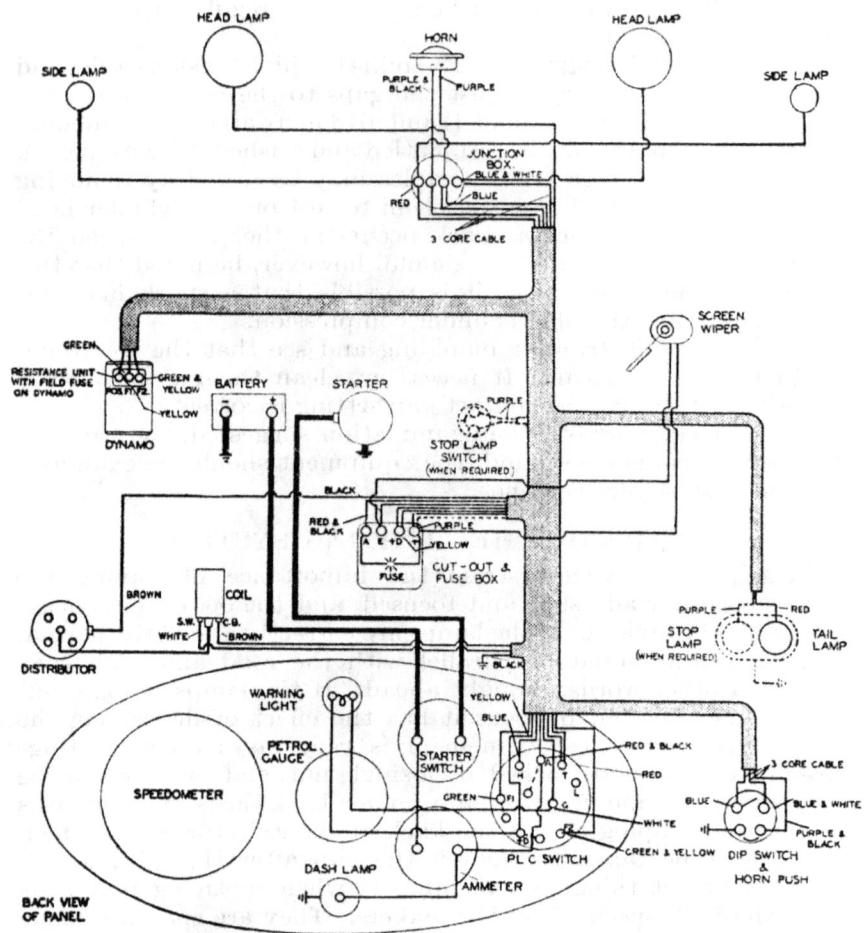

FIG. 55. LIGHTING, STARTING, AND COIL IGNITION WIRING DIAGRAM

THE ELECTRICAL EQUIPMENT 103

Dashlamp. This operates by turning the knurled cover of the lamp which operates the switch. Withdraw the cover when it becomes necessary to replace the bulb. When replacing the cover make sure that the small stud is placed opposite the slot in the base.

Electric Horn. The horn is carefully adjusted before leaving the makers and should not be interfered with. Should it fail to function or become intermittent in action, make sure that the trouble is not due to a loose connection in the wiring, run-down battery, or a blown fuse. If an alteration of the note is noticed, this may be due to the horn becoming loose on the mounting.

Wiring. Periodically examine all the wiring of the car in order to make sure that it has not come adrift or is rubbing on parts of the chassis or body. Should any signs of chafing of wires be noticed, tape all such places with good quality black tape. Do not allow oil to stay on the wiring.

RUNNING INSTRUCTIONS AND MAINTENANCE

The Battery. It is of the utmost importance that the battery should receive regular attention, as upon its good condition depend the satisfactory running of the starting motor, the current for the lamps, and the running of the car.

The following are the most important maintenance hints—

1. Keep the acid level with the tops of the separators.
2. Add only distilled water, never tap water.
3. Test the condition of the battery by taking readings of the specific gravity of the acid with a hydrometer.
4. Never leave the battery in a discharged condition.
5. Keep the terminals spanner tight and smeared with vaseline. Also, with earth return sets, see that the nut securing the lead from the negative battery terminal to the chassis is tight.

Topping-up. At least once a month remove the vent plugs in the top of the battery and examine the level of the acid solution. If necessary, add distilled water, which can be obtained at all chemists and most garages, to bring the acid level with the tops of the separators. If acid solution has been spilled, it must be replaced by a diluted sulphuric acid solution of the strength indicated on either the side or the cover of the battery. When examining the cells, naked lights must not be held near the vents, on account of the possible danger of igniting the gas coming from the plates.

Greasing Terminals. Examine the battery terminals and see that they are quite tight. Keep them smeared with vaseline to prevent corrosion. Keep the top of the battery clean and dry; take care not to spill water on it when adjusting the level of the electrolyte or taking specific gravity readings.

Testing the Condition of the Battery. It is advisable to complete the inspection by measuring the specific gravity of the acid, as this gives a very good indication of the state of charge of the battery.

An instrument known as a hydrometer is employed for this purpose, and is obtainable from Messrs. Lucas. Voltmeter readings of each cell do not provide a reliable indication of the condition of the battery unless special precautions are taken which make such a test unsuitable for the average owner, and on that account this test is not recommended.

How to Use the Hydrometer. Before measuring the specific gravity of the acid solution by means of the hydrometer, see that the acid is at its correct level. Readings should be taken for each of the cells in turn after a run on the car, when the electrolyte is thoroughly mixed. The readings should be approximately the same. If one cell gives a reading very different from the rest it may be that the acid has been spilled or has leaked from this particular cell, or there may be a short between the plates. In this case I advise the owner to have his battery examined at a Lucas Service Depot to trace the cause and prevent the trouble from developing.

Specific gravity readings and their indications are as follows— 1·285–1·300 battery fully charged, about 1·210 battery half discharged, and about 1·150 battery fully discharged. These figures are given assuming the temperature of the solution is about 60° F.

If the battery is found to be in a half-discharged or lower state of charge, leave the charging switch, if possible, in the full-charge position for longer periods of running (see opposite page). It should be remembered that the battery will be helped to regain its normal condition if its load is temporarily lessened, as, for instance, by using the side- instead of the headlamps. If the gravity does not rise in a reasonable time, it is advisable to have the battery inspected at a Lucas Service Depot. On the other hand, if the battery is always found to be in a fully-charged condition and the acid level gets unusually low, then decrease the charging time.

The battery must never be left in a fully-discharged condition, and unless some long runs are to be taken it is advisable to have the battery charged up from an independent electrical supply.

Storage of a Battery. If the equipment is not used for several months, the battery must be given a small charge from a separate source of electrical energy about once a fortnight, in order to obviate any permanent sulphation of the plates. In no circumstances must the electrolyte be removed from the battery and

THE ELECTRICAL EQUIPMENT

the plates allowed to dry, as certain changes take place which result in loss of capacity.

Use of the Battery Charging Switch. The battery is the "reservoir" for the energy generated by the dynamo and once it is "full" there is no object in delivering further current to it. While it is always better to keep a battery overcharged rather than undercharged, it should be remembered that excessive overcharging will quickly reduce the acid level and tend to shorten the life of the battery.

In summer, when the lamps are very little used, keep the switch in the "half-charge" position; and in winter, when the lighting and starting load is heavier, keep the switch in "full-charge" position. For cars running under average conditions, this will ensure that the battery is kept in a fully-charged state.

However, in exceptional cases it may be advisable to use the switches out of season. For instance, if in winter the car is run regularly during the day with practically no night running, and the hydrometer readings are always found to be about 1·285 and if the acid level gets unusually low, then it is probable that the battery is being overcharged. In these circumstances, move the charging switch to the half-charge position. On the other hand, if exceptional use is made of the lamps and starter in the summer, causing the battery to be in a low state of charge (hydrometer readings of 1·200 or under), then run with the charging switch in the full-charge position.

CHAPTER VIII

CARE OF TYRES

DUNLOP tyres are fitted as standard on all B.S.A. Three Wheelers, and it is advisable to refit with the same make of tyre.

In the manufacture of Dunlop tyres, the results of a considerable amount of research, experiment, and testing are embodied, and the tyre is designed to give the maximum degree of comfort and reliability.

To obtain the best results, it is suggested that the recommendations which follow should be adopted. The tyre is a pneumatic tyre, i.e. the fundamental basis of its design is the employment of air at a carefully regulated pressure.

Air is a gas, and like all other gases, is extremely resilient and mobile. It is, therefore, able to provide a very high degree of cushioning and also to conform readily to the varying shapes of a flexible container. If compressed air is to be used in this way, it is necessary to have a strong and flexible container which will prevent losses of air, will imprison the pressure and will, at the same time, permit the greatest possible cushioning to be obtained from the flexibility of the gas.

The inner tube is, of course, the part of the tyre intended to prevent leakage of air. Although entirely non-porous, there is some little loss of air due to a physical process known as "diffusion." The loss, however, only amounts to about 1 to 3 lb. per sq. in. each week, and as the air becomes staler the rate of loss diminishes.

The cover is of sufficient strength to retain the pressure, is flexible so that as little as possible of the resilience of air may be lost, and is endowed with tread and wall rubbers designed to provide adequate non-skidding properties and longevity.

The tyres are of the wired type mounted on well-base rims, a rubber rim band being fitted in the base of the rim to prevent any chafing between the tube and the spoke heads.

IMPORTANCE OF CORRECT INFLATION

It will be realized at once that the correct maintenance of the required air pressures is the main secret of successful tyre usage and long tyre life.

The recommended inflation pressures for the tyres fitted to B.S.A. Three Wheelers are shown on the opposite page.

There is really no excuse for running tyres in an under-inflated

CARE OF TYRES

state, because air costs nothing and the effort required to keep pressures right is so little.

Tyre Size	Front	Rear
	(lb. per sq. in.)	
4.00 in. × 19 in.	22	28
3.50 in. × 18 in.	20	26

The above table pressures are for normal loads. Increase the pressures when the load is above normal.

The valve of the Schrader type automatically allows the flow of air into the tyre from the pump and also automatically closes the valve when the flow ceases. The fitting of the valve cap—the secondary seal—guarantees the valve airtight to a pressure of 250 lb. per sq. in. The valve, however, can be opened when

FIG. 56. DUNLOP NO. 1 PENCIL TYPE GAUGE

it is desired to check pressures or to reduce pressures by depressing the small pin which is seen in the valve aperture. There is no difficulty therefore in checking pressures. A gauge which fits directly to the valve should always be used to make quite sure that the reading is that of the air pressure within the tyre. Gauges on pumps, while reliable indicators of pressures at the point where they are inserted, may not give a correct reading of the pressure within the tyre.

Gauges are comparatively inexpensive, and the Dunlop Gauge (Fig. 56), which is shaped like a pencil, has a small clip for the vest pocket. Both the valve inside mechanism and the valve cap have rubber washers, and as these may be subject to some deterioration, it is advisable to replace them with new ones once a year.

The maintenance of the correct pressure being important, what then are the effects of insufficient pressure?

Under-inflation reduces tyre life by adversely affecting both casing and tread.

In an under-inflated tyre the casing is made to bend to a very much greater extent than is intended, and the bending is greatest at a particular point on the shoulder (upper wall) on each side of the cover. When a cover bends, each layer of the casing is compelled to move in relation to every other layer. Adhesion is maintained by the elastic rubber in which each cord and each layer of cords is embedded. Excessive movement of this rubber produces internal friction and this, together with the constant bending of the cords themselves, results in the generation of high temperatures and fatigue of the material. As a consequence, one or more of the casing cords may break and this will gradually cause the breaking-up of the casing itself along the shoulders.

Next, consider for a moment the condition of an under-inflated tyre which is subjected to a very heavy and localized blow. The tyre is in the shape, sectionally, of a circle, and therefore the inner plies or layers of the casing are of shorter length than the outer ones. If a sharp localized blow is received by an under-inflated tyre, the casing is bent inwards sharply and quickly at one spot, with the result that the inner layers are constantly called upon to achieve a very great increase in their length. The result is that a heavy blow may cause the casing of an under-inflated tyre to fracture. The fracture will chafe the tube and bring about deflation.

The contour of a tyre tread and the displacement of the rubber mass is designed to give even wear throughout the whole life of the tyre while used at correct pressures. If the pressures are inadequate the tyre tread lacks support. The first effect of this is that the centre of the tread retreats and the sides of the tread have to bear all the weight and the stresses. They will consequently be worn away at a rate very much in excess of that experienced by the centre of the tread. The fact that the load is being transmitted through the tyre will also cause each stud of the tread to be excessively distorted and become quite out of shape while under load. The rubber, however, will have a natural tendency to return to its original shape. When, therefore (as the tyre moves forward) sufficient load has passed off the stud so that it is no longer capable of withstanding the pull of the rubber, the stud will spring back to its original shape, while some load still remains upon it, and the trailing end of the stud will consequently be worn away by abrasion with the road. This kind of wear is sometimes referred to as "heel and toe" wear.

Over-inflation is also to be avoided because the casing may be crushed if a heavy blow is received, and as the tyre is more likely to bounce over irregularities in the road, abrasive wear due to the tyre spinning may be caused.

Wheel Alinement

Sometimes road wheels may be thrown out of alinement either by a sharp blow or by frequent contact with kerbs. Most garages possess alinement gauges and it is a good plan to have the alinement (particularly of the front wheels) checked occasionally.

CARE OF TYRES

If the wheels are not in correct alinement, then, obviously, the wheels are not turning in the same direction as the car is travelling. This causes very severe abrasive wear of the tyres.

The importance of quite small errors can be gauged by the fact that an *error* in the alinement of a wheel of $\frac{1}{8}$ in. is equivalent in its effect to placing the wheel at right angles to the vehicle and keeping it spinning in that position for 9 yd. in every mile. No one would do this deliberately, yet many suffer it unconsciously.

If it is noticed that on the tread of the tyre there is a fine upstanding "lip" at the edge of any of the studs or blocks which

FIG. 57. ONE METHOD OF TESTING WHEEL ALINEMENT

form the pattern, or that the surface of the rubber presents a slightly grained or filed appearance, misalinement should at once be suspected and no delay take place of having the alinement checked and corrected.

In the same way, if there are any loosenesses in the steering mechanism or the wheel bearings, these will allow the wheels to wander from side to side and cause intermittent misalinement with its attendant ill-effects.

DRIVING

Methods of driving do make a difference to tyre wear. Excessive acceleration and harsh braking both cause slip between the tyre and the road. The rate of wear is roughly proportional to the square of the slip and the practice of using the foot heavily on either the accelerator or brake pedals must undoubtedly cause a reduction of tyre life. In emergency, it is necessary to do this, but, as a general rule, the smoother the start or the halt, the longer will the tyres last.

Kerbs, tramlines, and railway points should be avoided. A sharp glancing blow against a kerb may damage the wall rubber, and has been known to cause a casing fracture where pressures are inadequate.

Tramlines and either tramline or railway points result in the weight on the tyre being concentrated in a small area, and if there should be any sharpness either of the rails or the points, the tyre may be severely cut.

The tyres should be protected from oil and grease, which have a detrimental effect upon rubber. Paraffin in particular is almost instantaneous in its action. It is well, therefore, to keep garage floors as clean as possible. Should any oil or grease get on to the tyres, it may be removed by the sparing use of petrol and a clean rag.

Repairs and Storage

Any small cuts which affect the rubber only should be filled in with a tread cut filling, as supplied by tyre manufacturers, after any stones or flints have been removed. Where, however, the damage affects the cotton part of the structure, the work should be carried out either by the tyre manufacturer or an expert vulcanizer having proper plant for the purpose. If the repairs are carried out promptly there is no reason why the potential life of the tyre should be affected. If, however, cuts which penetrate to the casing are neglected, water and road-matter penetrate through, deterioration sets in, the damage extends, and usually the cover cannot be repaired satisfactorily.

During overhauls it is advisable to remove entirely all the tyres from the rims. If the rims are rusted, a coat of rubber non-oily paint should be applied.

The cover and tube may then be thoroughly examined, and any cuts or damage which have not previously been noticed may then be repaired. This will ensure that the tyres are in really good condition when the car is taken out on the road again.

If the car is laid up for a period, the tyres should be protected from light, heat, damp, oil, and grease. The best plan is to remove them entirely from the car and wrap them in paper, and hang them up in a dry cool place. If this is not possible, then the car should be jacked up off the tyres and steps taken to diminish the amount of light reaching them by throwing a sheet of brown paper, or similar substance, over each tyre. An alternative method is to keep the tyres strictly inflated to the required pressure and to change the position of the wheels occasionally so that the car is not always standing on the same portion of tyre.

CARE OF TYRES

Fitting and Removal Instructions

It should be noted that *inextensible* wires are incorporated in the edges of wired type tyres (see Fig. 58). Therefore, do not attempt to stretch the wire edges of the tyre cover over the rim edge.

Force is entirely unnecessary and may be dangerous, as it merely tends to damage the cover edges and serves no helpful purpose.

Fitting or removing will be quite easy if the wire edges are carefully adjusted into the rim base; if it is not found to be easy, the operation is not being correctly performed.

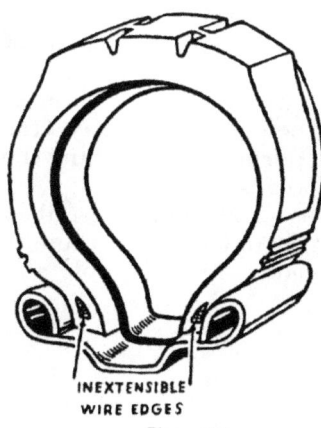

Fig. 58

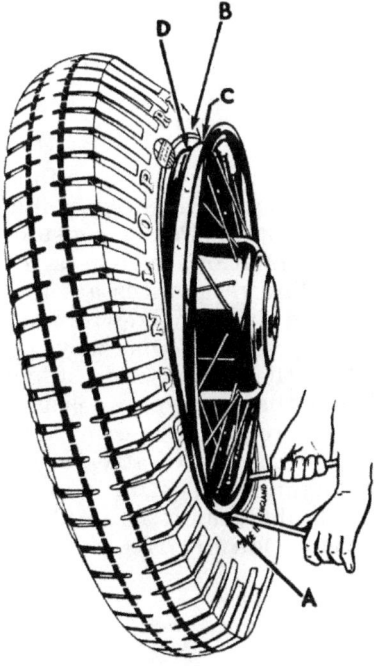

Fig. 59. Showing Method of Removing Tyre

To Remove Tyre. Remove all valve parts and push both cover edges into the base of the rim at the part diametrically opposite the valve, then lever the cover edges near the valve over the rim edge.

You cannot pull the cover edge at A (Fig. 59) over the rim edge until the cover edge at B is pushed off the rim shoulder C down into the well D, then the cover edge at A comes over the rim easily. Remember, the cover edges are inextensible—force will only damage the cover and cannot stretch the edge.

To Fit Tyre. Push one edge of the cover over the edge of the rim. It will go quite easily if the part first put on is pushed right down into the rim base.

Very slightly inflate the inner tube—do not distend it—place it in the cover, with the valve through the hole in the rim. (Take care that the valve, which is fitted in the side of the tube, is on the correct side of the rim.)

Fit the second edge of the cover, commencing at a point diametrically opposite the valve, and pushing the edge down into the base of the rim.

Small levers may be gently used to ease the last few inches over the rim edge.

While inflating, see that the edges of the cover are seated evenly round the rim.

Reduction of Costs

If the above hints are followed, it will be obvious that no tyre wastage will take place and that tyre costs will be reduced to a minimum. Petrol consumption may also be reduced because under-inflation increases considerably the rolling resistance. If rolling resistances are increased, then petrol consumption for a given journey likewise increases.

In just the same way, there is a definite drag on the wheels when they are not in alinement, and then it is perfectly true to say that more petrol is used for the sole purpose of providing the energy required to grind away the tyre treads.

The amount of attention which tyres need, although described in detail here, is, in sum total, very little indeed, and there is no doubt that it is amply repaid by freedom from trouble and a reduction in costs.

APPENDIX

USEFUL INFORMATION AND TABLES

EQUIVALENT SPEEDS

| Time for 1 Mile || Speeds ||
Minutes	Seconds	Miles per Hour	Kilometres per Hour
1	0	60·00	96·51
1	5	55·43	89·10
1	10	51·42	82·73
1	15	47·99	77·21
1	20	45·00	72·40
1	25	42·36	68·14
1	30	40·00	64·36
1	35	37·89	60·96
1	40	36·00	57·92
1	45	34·29	55·16
1	50	32·73	52·65
2	0	30·00	48·26
2	20	25·71	41·36
2	40	22·50	36·20
3	0	20·00	32·18
3	20	18·00	28·96
3	30	17·14	27·58
3	40	16·36	26·32
3	50	15·60	25·18
4	0	15·00	24·13

EQUIVALENTS OF KILOMETRES IN MILES

Kilometres	Miles	Kilometres	Miles	Kilometres	Miles
0·805	½	11·265	7	80·466	50
1·609	1	12·875	8	96·558	60
3·219	2	14·484	9	112·652	70
4·828	3	16·093	10	128·744	80
6·437	4	32·186	20	144·838	90
8·047	5	48·279	30	160·931	100
9·656	6	64·372	40		

EQUIVALENTS OF DEGREES FAHRENHEIT AND CENTIGRADE

Fahr.	Cent.	Fahr.	Cent.	Fahr.	Cent.
32·0*	0*	59·0	15	100·4	38
33·8	1	68·0	20	104·0	40
35·6	2	77·0	25	122·0	50
41·0	5	86·0	30	212·0†	100†
50·0	10	95·0	35		

* Freezing point of water.   † Boiling point of water.

FORMULA FOR ASCERTAINING THE CUBIC CAPACITY OF AN ENGINE

$$D^2 \times N \times S \times ·7854$$

where D = cylinder bore; N = number of cylinders; S = stroke.

Example. To find cubic capacity of a four-cylinder 75 × 110 mm. engine—

$$75 \times 75 \times 4 \times 110 \times ·7854$$

R.A.C. (TREASURY) H.P. FORMULA

Measurement in Inches.   Measurement in Millimetres.

$$\frac{D^2 \times N}{2·5} \qquad \qquad \frac{D^2 \times N}{1613}$$

where D = cylinder bore; N = number of cylinders.

This formula assumes a constant piston speed of 1000 ft. per minute and a mean effective pressure (M.E.P.) of 67·2 lb. per sq. in., both being admittedly much below the average of modern engines.

SOME USEFUL ROAD MILEAGES (Approximate)

	Aberdeen	Birmingham	Bristol	Cambridge	Cardiff	Derby	Dover	Edinburgh	Exeter	Glasgow	Gloucester	Hull	Inverness	Lancaster	Leeds	Leicester	Lincoln	Liverpool	London	Manchester	Oxford	Penzance	Scarborough	Sheffield	Southampton
Aberdeen	—	408	491	462	499	385	580	112	540	142	456	348	105	271	322	412	386	388	509	340	520	644	312	370	516
Birmingham	408	—	85	99	101	39	181	281	156	294	52	144	459	119	107	36	88	86	110	80	62	260	158	72	125
Bristol	491	85	—	139	96	125	194	369	70	364	34	224	518	206	190	118	170	176	119	152	67	174	243	160	68
Cambridge	462	99	139	—	172	96	124	348	209	367	140	129	516	176	144	64	86	187	53	152	82	339	172	116	151
Cardiff	499	101	96	172	—	141	232	377	160	382	57	240	533	209	206	132	184	154	160	168	104	270	268	176	152
Derby	385	39	125	96	141	—	198	273	206	274	91	92	430	114	69	28	52	82	127	62	101	319	124	36	158
Dover	580	181	194	124	232	198	—	468	236	467	172	290	624	307	263	174	205	274	71	259	126	351	311	234	140
Edinburgh	112	281	369	348	377	273	468	—	439	44	334	236	156	162	208	315	264	209	397	209	393	552	200	236	457
Exeter	540	156	70	209	166	206	236	439	—	440	102	306	594	282	256	208	260	222	169	224	134	104	348	226	100
Glasgow	142	294	364	367	382	274	467	44	440	—	335	251	167	160	209	306	277	212	396	210	360	553	235	242	419
Gloucester	456	52	34	140	57	91	172	334	102	335	—	190	483	161	163	78	146	124	102	134	50	220	215	120	112
Hull	348	144	224	129	240	92	290	236	306	251	190	—	382	121	58	124	96	128	219	100	175	419	43	64	230
Inverness	105	459	518	516	533	430	624	156	594	167	483	383	—	312	365	467	442	380	553	380	521	713	357	113	584
Lancaster	271	119	206	179	209	114	307	162	282	160	161	121	312	—	67	138	139	53	236	56	184	391	126	90	248
Leeds	322	107	190	144	206	69	263	208	256	209	163	58	365	67	—	90	68	72	192	46	169	389	65	30	229
Leicester	412	36	118	64	132	28	174	315	208	306	78	124	467	138	90	—	52	119	98	84	64	312	145	60	124
Lincoln	386	88	170	86	184	52	205	264	260	277	146	96	442	139	68	52	—	110	134	92	126	378	109	44	175
Liverpool	388	86	176	187	154	82	274	209	222	212	124	128	380	53	72	119	110	—	201	35	149	326	139	72	223
London	509	110	119	53	160	127	71	397	169	396	102	219	553	236	192	98	134	201	—	188	55	278	240	162	76
Manchester	340	80	152	152	168	62	259	209	224	210	134	100	380	56	46	84	92	35	188	—	148	352	108	36	208
Oxford	520	62	67	82	104	101	126	393	134	360	50	175	521	184	169	64	126	149	55	148	—	245	—	124	64
Penzance	644	260	174	339	270	319	351	552	104	553	220	419	713	391	389	312	378	326	278	352	245	—	443	—	221
Scarborough	312	158	243	172	268	124	311	200	348	235	215	43	357	126	65	145	109	139	240	108	232	443	—	94	282
Sheffield	370	72	160	116	176	36	234	236	226	242	120	64	113	90	30	60	44	72	162	36	124	—	94	—	195
Southampton	516	125	68	151	152	158	140	457	100	419	112	230	584	248	229	124	175	223	76	208	64	221	282	195	—

FUEL AND OIL
RUNNING EXPENSES

Date	Petrol		Oil		Speedo-meter Reading	M.P.G.	
	Gallons	£ s. d.	Pints	£ s. d.		Petrol	Oil

FUEL AND OIL
RUNNING EXPENSES

Date	Petrol		Oil		Speedo-meter Reading	M.P.G.	
	Gallons	£ s. d.	Pints	£ s. d.		Petrol	Oil

FUEL AND OIL
RUNNING EXPENSES

Date	PETROL		OIL		Speedo-meter Reading	M.P.G.	
	Gallons	£ s. d.	Pints	£ s. d.		Petrol	Oil

FUEL AND OIL
RUNNING EXPENSES

Date	Petrol		Oil		Speedo-meter Reading	M.P.G.	
	Gallons	£ s. d.	Pints	£ s. d.		Petrol	Oil

INDEX

ACCELERATION, 77
Accidents, what to do, 14
Adjusting carburettor, 64
—— clutch, 69
—— dynamo chain, 60
—— shock absorbers, 70
Attention to pistons and rings, 56

BADGES, 75
Battery charging switch, use of, 105
—— maintenance, 103
—— storage, 105
—— terminals, greasing, 103
—— testing, 104
Bodywork, 6
Boiling in radiator, 73
Brakes, adjusting, 69
——, use of, 30
Brushes, care of, 93

CARBURETTOR, 62
—— faults, 67
Care of the car, 29
—— of the lighting system, 101
—— of the tyres, 106
—— of the wings, 31
Causes of boiling, 73
Changing gear, 28
Chassis, 69
—— lubrication, 88
Chromium plating, care of, 31
Cleaning petrol filter, 73
Clutch, adjusting, 69
Coil ignition system, maintenance of, 95
Commutator, cleaning, 93
Contact-breaker, 34, 48
Correct valve setting, 61
Cylinder removal, 37
—— head removal, 52

DASHLAMP, 103
Decarbonizing, 40, 53

Description of lubrication system, 80
Diagnosing carburettor faults, 67
Differential lubrication, 87
Dismantling notes, 74
Distributor, lubrication of, 97
Driving, 27
—— licence, 10
—— ——, renewing, 11

ELECTRIC horn, 103
Electrical equipment, 92
Engine, removing, 75
—— troubles, 75
Examining and renewing piston rings, 41
Exhaust rocker-boxes, cleaning, 39

FIELD fuse, 94
Fitting new valve springs, 45
Float chamber removal, 63
Frame and suspension, 1
Fuel consumption, 78

GEARBOX lubrication, 87
—— removal, 74
Grinding-in valves, 43, 54

HEADLAMPS, 101
Hydrometer, using, 104

IGNITION faults, remedying, 98
—— lever, use of, 29
—— timing, 47, 57
—— warning light, 98
Insurance, 13

LAW, 14
Licences, 10
Lighting system, care of, 101
Lubrication, 80

MAIN jet size, 67

INDEX

Maintenance and overhaul, 3
Misfiring and bad starting, 101

OIL level, 85
—— recommendations, 91
On the road with the Three Wheeler, 21
"Otto" Cycle, 18
Overheating, 78

PEDAL board, removing, 74
Petrol filter, cleaning, 73
Piston removal, 38
—— ring removal, 41
Poor acceleration, 77

RADIATOR, 72
——, precautions against freezing, 73
——, removing, 74
Range of models, 1
Registration of the car, 12
Removing cylinders, 37
—— cylinder head, 52
—— pistons, 38, 56
—— rear wheel arm, 75
Running-in new engines, 29

SHOCK absorber adjustment, 70
Slow running adjustment, 66

Sparking plugs, 32, 47
Springs, lubrication of, 91
Starter motor, care of, 94
Steering gear, 72
Storing the battery, 105
Summary of engine troubles, 75

TAPPET adjustment, 35, 48
Testing condition of battery, 104
—— valves after grinding-in, 44
Theory of the four-stroke engine, 16
Timing the ignition, 47, 57
—— the valves, 61
Topping-up the battery, 103
Tuning carburettor for power, 66
Tyres, care of, 106
——, recommended pressures, 107

USE of brakes, 30
—— of ignition lever, 29

VALVE removal, 38, 52
—— timing, 61

WATER hose connections, 73
—— level in radiator, 73
Wheel removal, 71
When to decarbonize, 37, 51
Wiring diagram, 102

AUTOBOOKS WORKSHOP MANUALS

ALFA ROMEO GIULIA 1300, 1600, 1750, 2000 1962-1978 WSM
BMW 1600 1966-1973 WSM
BMW 2500, 2800, 3.0 & 3.3 1968-1977 WSM
BMW 316, 320, 320i 1975-1977 WSM
BMW 518, 520, 520i 1973-1981 WSM
FIAT 1100, 1100D, 1100R & 1200 1957-1969 WSM
FIAT 124 1966-1974 WSM
FIAT 124 SPORT 1966-1975 WSM
FIAT 125 & 125 SPECIAL 1967-1973 WSM
FIAT 126, 126L, 126 DV, 126/650 & 126/650 DV 1972-1982 WSM
FIAT 127 SALOON, SPECIAL & SPORT, 900, 1050 1971-1981 WSM
FIAT 128 1969-1982 WSM
FIAT 1300, 1500 1961-1967 WSM
FIAT 131 MIRAFIORI 1975-1982 WSM
FIAT 132 1972-1982 WSM
FIAT 500 1957-1973 WSM
FIAT 600, 600D & MULTIPLA 1955-1969 WSM
FIAT 850 1964-1972 WSM
JAGUAR MK 1, 2 1955-1969 WSM
JAGUAR S TYPE, 420 1963-1968 WSM
JAGUAR XK 120, 140, 150 MK 7, 8, 9 1948-1961 WSM
LAND ROVER 1, 2 1948-1961 WSM
MERCEDES-BENZ 190 1959-1968 WSM
MERCEDES-BENZ 220/8 1968-1972 WSM
MERCEDES-BENZ 220B 1959-1965 WSM
MERCEDES-BENZ 230 1963-1968 WSM
MERCEDES-BENZ 250 1968-1972 WSM
MERCEDES-BENZ 280 1968-1972 WSM
MINI 1959-1980 WSM
MORRIS MINOR 1952-1971 WSM
PEUGEOT 404 1960-1975 WSM
PORSCHE 911 1964-1973 WSM
PORSCHE 911 1970-1977 WSM
RENAULT 16 1965-1979 WSM
RENAULT 8, 10, 1100 1962-1971 WSM
ROVER 3500, 3500S 1968-1976 WSM
SUNBEAM RAPIER, ALPINE 1955-1965 WSM
TRIUMPH SPITFIRE, GT6, VITESSE 1962-1968 WSM
TRIUMPH TR4, TR4A 1961-1967 WSM
VOLKSWAGEN BEETLE 1968-1977 WSM

VELOCEPRESS AUTOMOBILE BOOKS & MANUALS

ABARTH BUYERS GUIDE
AUSTIN-HEALEY 6-CYLINDER WSM
AUSTIN-HEALEY SPRITE & MG MIDGET 1958-1971 WSM
BMW 600 LIMOUSINE FACTORY WSM
BMW 600 LIMOUSINE OWNERS HAND BOOK & SERVICE MANUAL
BMW 2000 & 2002 1966-1976 WSM
BMW ISETTA FACTORY WSM
CARRERA PANAMERICANA - MEXICAN ROAD RACE (BOOK OF)
COMPLETE CATALOG OF JAPANESE MOTOR VEHICLES
CORVAIR 1960-1969 OWNERS WORKSHOP MANUAL
CORVETTE V8 1955-1962 OWNERS WORKSHOP MANUAL
DIALED IN - THE JAN OPPERMAN STORY
FERRARI 250/GT SERVICE AND MAINTENANCE
FERRARI 308 SERIES BUYER'S AND OWNER'S GUIDE
FERRARI BERLINETTA LUSSO
FERRARI BROCHURES AND SALES LITERATURE 1946-1967
FERRARI BROCHURES AND SALES LITERATURE 1968-1989
FERRARI GUIDE TO PERFORMANCE
FERRARI OPP, MAINTENANCE & SERVICE H/BOOKS 1948-1963
FERRARI OWNER'S HANDBOOK
FERRARI SERIAL NUMBERS PART I - ODD NUMBERS TO 21399
FERRARI SERIAL NUMBERS PART II - EVEN NUMBERS TO 1050
FERRARI SPYDER CALIFORNIA
FERRARI TUNING TIPS & MAINTENANCE TECHNIQUES
HENRY'S FABULOUS MODEL "A" FORD
HOW TO BUILD A FIBERGLASS CAR
HOW TO BUILD A RACING CAR
HOW TO RESTORE THE MODEL 'A' FORD
IF HEMINGWAY HAD WRITTEN A RACING NOVEL
JAGUAR E-TYPE 3.8 & 4.2 WSM
LE MANS 24 (THE BOOK THAT THE FILM WAS BASED ON)
MASERATI BROCHURES AND SALES LITERATURE
MASERATI OWNER'S HANDBOOK
METROPOLITAN FACTORY WSM
MGA & MGB OWNERS HANDBOOK & WSM
MG MIDGET TC, TD, TF & TF1500 WORKSHOP MANUAL
OBERT'S FIAT GUIDE
PERFORMANCE TUNING THE SUNBEAM TIGER
PORSCHE 356 1948-1965 WSM
PORSCHE 912 WSM
SOUPING THE VOLKSWAGEN
SOLEX CARBURETORS (EMPHASIS ON UK & EU AUTOMOBILES)
SU CARBURETORS (EMPHASIS ON UK AUTOMOBILES)
TRIUMPH TR2, TR3, TR4 1953-1965 WSM
TUNING FOR SPEED (P.E. IRVING)
VEDA ORR'S NEW REVISED HOT ROD PICTORIAL
VOLKSWAGEN TRANSPORTER, TRUCKS, STATION WAGONS WSM
VOLVO 1944-1968 ALL MODELS WSM
WEBER CARBURETORS (EMPHASIS ON ALFA & FIAT)

VELOCEPRESS THREE WHEELER BOOKS & MANUALS

BSA THREE WHEELER (BOOK OF)

BROOKLANDS BOOKS & ROAD TEST PORTFOLIOS (RTP)

AC CARS 1904-2009
ALFA ROMEO 1920-1933 ROAD TEST PORTFOLIO
ALFA ROMEO 1934-1940 ROAD TEST PORTFOLIO
BRABHAM RALT HONDA THE RON TAURANAC STORY
BUGATTI TYPE 10 TO TYPE 40 ROAD TEST PORTFOLIO
BUGATTI TYPE 10 TO TYPE 251 ROAD TEST PORTFOLIO
BUGATTI TYPE 41 TO TYPE 55 ROAD TEST PORTFOLIO
BUGATTI TYPE 57 TO TYPE 251 ROAD TEST PORTFOLIO
DELAHAYE ROAD TEST PORTFOLIO
FERRARI ROAD CARS 1946-1956 ROAD TEST PORTFOLIO
FIAT 500 1936-1972 ROAD TEST PORTFOLIO
FIAT DINO ROAD TEST PORTFOLIO
HISPANO SUIZA ROAD TEST PORTFOLIO
HONDA ST1100/ST1300 PAN EUROPEAN 1990-2002 RTP
JAGUAR MK1 & MK2 ROAD TEST PORTFOLIO
LOTUS CORTINA ROAD TEST PORTFOLIO
MV AGUSTA F4 750 & 1000 1997-2007 ROAD TEST PORTFOLIO
TATRA CARS ROAD TEST PORTFOLIO

VELOCEPRESS MOTORCYCLE BOOKS & MANUALS

1930'S BRITISH MOTORCYCLE CARBS & ELEC COMPONENTS (BOOK OF)
1930'S BRITISH MOTORCYCLE GEARBOXES & CLUTCHES (BOOK OF)
AJS SINGLES & TWINS 250cc THRU 1000cc 1932-1948 (BOOK OF)
AJS SINGLES 1955-65 350cc & 500cc (BOOK OF)
AJS SINGLES 1945-60 350cc & 500cc MODELS 16 & 18 (BOOK OF)
ARIEL 1939-1960 4 STROKE SINGLES (BOOK OF)
ARIEL LEADER & ARROW 1958-1964 (BOOK OF)
ARIEL MOTORCYCLES 1933-1951 WSM
ARIEL PREWAR MODELS 1932-1939 (BOOK OF)
BMW M/CYCLES R26 R27 (1956-1967) FACTORY WSM
BMW M/CYCLES R50 R50S R60 R69S (1955-1969) FACTORY WSM
BSA BANTAM ALL MODELS FROM 1948 ONWARDS (BOOK OF)
BSA SINGLES & V-TWINS UP TO 1927 (BOOK OF)
BSA SINGLES & V-TWINS 1936-1939 (BOOK OF)
BSA SINGLES & V-TWINS 1936-1952 (BOOK OF)
BSA OHV & SV SINGLES 250-600cc 1945-1954 (BOOK OF)
BSA OHV & SV SINGLES - 250cc 1954-1970 (BOOK OF)
BSA OHV SINGLES 350 & 500cc 1955-1967 (BOOK OF)
BSA TWINS 1948-1962 (BOOK OF)
BSA TWINS 1962-1969 (SECOND BOOK OF)
CATALOG OF BRITISH MOTORCYCLES (1951 MODELS)
DOUGLAS PRE-WAR ALL MODELS 1929-1939 (BOOK OF)
DOUGLAS POST-WAR ALL MODELS 1948-1957 FACTORY WSM
DUCATI 160cc, 250cc & 350cc OHC MODELS FACTORY WSM
HONDA 50 ALL MODELS UP TO 1970 INC MONKEY & TRAIL (BOOK OF)
HONDA 90 ALL MODELS UP TO 1966 (BOOK OF)
HONDA MOTORCYCLES 125-150 TWINS C/CS/CB/CA WSM
HONDA MOTORCYCLES 250-305 TWINS C/CS/CB WSM
HONDA MOTORCYCLES C100 SUPER CUB WSM
HONDA MOTORCYCLES C110 SPORT CUB 1962-1969 WSM
HONDA TWINS & SINGLES 50cc THRU 305cc 1960-1966 (BOOK OF)
HONDA TWINS ALL MODELS 125cc THRU 450cc UP TO 1968 (BOOK OF)
INDIAN PONYBIKE, BOY RACER & PAPOOSE ILL PARTS LIST & SALES LIT
J.A.P. ENGINES 1927-1952 & MOTORCYCLES 1934-1952 (BOOK OF)
LAMBRETTA ALL 125 & 150cc MODELS 1947-1957 (BOOK OF)
LAMBRETTA LI & TV MODELS 1957-1970 (SECOND BOOK OF)
MATCHLESS 350 & 500cc SINGLES 1945-1956 (BOOK OF)
MATCHLESS 350 & 500cc SINGLES 1955-1966 (BOOK OF)
MOTORCYCLE ENGINEERING (P. E. Irving)
NORTON 1932-1947 (BOOK OF)
NORTON 1938-1956 (BOOK OF)
NORTON DOMINATOR TWINS 1955-1965 (BOOK OF)
NORTON MODELS 19, 50 & ES2 1955-1963 (BOOK OF)
NORTON MOTORCYCLES 1957-1970 FACTORY WSM
NORTON PREWAR MODELS 1932-1939 (BOOK OF)
NSU PRIMA ALL MODELS 1956-1964 (BOOK OF)
NSU QUICKLY ALL MODELS 1953-1963 (BOOK OF)
RALEIGH MOPEDS 1960-1969 (BOOK OF)
RALEIGH MOTORCYCLES 1919-1933 (BOOK OF)
ROYAL ENFIELD SINGLES & V TWINS 1934-1946 (BOOK OF)
ROYAL ENFIELD SINGLES & V TWINS 1937-1953 (BOOK OF)
ROYAL ENFIELD SINGLES 1946-1962 (BOOK OF)
ROYAL ENFIELD 736cc INTERCEPTOR FACTORY WSM
ROYAL ENFIELD 250cc & 350cc SINGLES 1958-1966 (SECOND BOOK OF)
RUDGE MOTORCYCLES 1933-1939 (BOOK OF)
SPEED AND HOW TO OBTAIN IT
SUNBEAM MOTORCYCLES 1928-1939 (BOOK OF)
SUNBEAM S7 & S8 1946-1957 (BOOK OF)
SUZUKI 50cc & 80cc UP TO 1966 (BOOK OF)
SUZUKI T10 1963-1967 FACTORY WSM
SUZUKI T20 & T200 1965-1969 FACTORY WSM
TRIUMPH PRE-WAR MOTORCYCLE 1935-1939 (BOOK OF)
TRIUMPH MOTORCYCLES 1935-1949 (BOOK OF)
TRIUMPH MOTORCYCLES 1937-1951 WSM
TRIUMPH MOTORCYCLES 1945-1955 FACTORY WSM
TRIUMPH TWINS 1945-1958 (BOOK OF)
TRIUMPH TWINS 1956-1969 (BOOK OF)
VELOCETTE ALL SINGLES & TWINS 1925-1970 (BOOK OF)
VESPA 1951-1961 (BOOK OF)
VESPA 125 & 150cc & GS MODELS 1955-1963 (SECOND BOOK OF)
VESPA 90, 125 & 150cc 1963-1972 (THIRD BOOK OF)
VESPA GS & SS 1955-1968 (BOOK OF)
VILLIERS ENGINE UP TO 1959 INC. 3 WHEELERS (BOOK OF)
VILLIERS ENGINE UP TO 1969 (BOOK OF)
VINCENT MOTORCYCLES 1935-1955 WSM

FOR A DETAILED DESCRIPTION OF ANY OF THESE TITLES PLEASE VISIT OUR WEBSITE www.VelocePress.com

www.ingramcontent.com/pod-product-compliance
Lightning Source LLC
Chambersburg PA
CBHW070555170426
43201CB00012B/1851